Cambridge Elements ≡

Elements in the Problems of God
edited by
Michael L. Peterson
Asbury Theological Seminary

GOD, RELIGIOUS EXTREMISM AND VIOLENCE

Matthew Rowley
Fairfield University

CAMBRIDGE
UNIVERSITY PRESS

CAMBRIDGE
UNIVERSITY PRESS

Shaftesbury Road, Cambridge CB2 8EA, United Kingdom

One Liberty Plaza, 20th Floor, New York, NY 10006, USA

477 Williamstown Road, Port Melbourne, VIC 3207, Australia

314–321, 3rd Floor, Plot 3, Splendor Forum, Jasola District Centre,
New Delhi – 110025, India

103 Penang Road, #05–06/07, Visioncrest Commercial, Singapore 238467

Cambridge University Press is part of Cambridge University Press & Assessment,
a department of the University of Cambridge.

We share the University's mission to contribute to society through the pursuit of
education, learning and research at the highest international levels of excellence.

www.cambridge.org
Information on this title: www.cambridge.org/9781009494427

DOI: 10.1017/9781009272315

First published 2024

A catalogue record for this publication is available from the British Library.

ISBN 978-1-009-49442-7 Hardback
ISBN 978-1-009-27230-8 Paperback
ISSN 2754-8724 (online)
ISSN 2754-8716 (print)

God, Religious Extremism and Violence

Elements in the Problems of God

DOI: 10.1017/9781009272315
First published online: February 2024

Matthew Rowley
Fairfield University

Author for correspondence: Matthew Rowley, mrowley@fairfield.edu

Abstract: Why do religious militants think their actions are right or righteous? What keeps me from acting like them? Why do some religious people act on their beliefs in charitable, inspiring and deeply humane ways? Is secularism the solution to religious violence, or is it part of the problem? This Element explores the vexed issue of violence done in the name of God, looking at the topic through the lens of peace and conflict studies, religious studies and historical studies. The beliefs of various communities, religious and secular, are explored, looking at how convictions inhibit and enable violence. This Element aims to foster a deeper and more nuanced understanding of the promises and perils of religion so that readers can better respond to a world filled with violence.

This Element also has a video abstract: www.cambridge.org/Rowley

Keywords: religion, secularism, violence, extremism, peacebuilding

ISBNs: 9781009494427 (HB), 9781009272308 (PB), 9781009272315 (OC)
ISSNs: 2754-8724 (online), 2754-8716 (print)

Contents

1 Does Religious Belief Matter?

The line separating a scholar of religious violence from a perpetrator is uncomfortably thin. I started university at a rural ministerial training school. A few professors were verbally combative when they denounced heresy, cults and non-Christian faiths. Some also derided America's liberal denominations. A few months after graduation, a student torched a nearby Episcopal church and was sentenced to thirteen years in prison. He had previously threatened another church, stolen from it, blamed the congregants for provoking God's wrath and then set the church ablaze after removing anything sacred (i.e. Bibles and the American flag). The arsonist called himself 'Shagmar' (Judg. 3:31), a biblical warrior. This arsonist demonstrates a key feature of violence in God's name: destruction often occurs within a religion (Stark and Corcoran 2014: 41), in this case, between rival Protestant groups.

I was jolted by another headline in 2020. Jewish Americans account for less than 3 per cent of the American population but suffer more than half of all religiously motivated hate crimes. An arsonist filled a canister with gasoline and used an evangelistic pamphlet as a wick. He placed the firebomb outside a Jewish nursing home. His incendiary device failed, and he was sentenced to ten years. I played after school with the arsonist. We attended the same Christian elementary school. We were in the same carpool. I was surprised by the arsonist's identity because I never thought of him as a committed Christian, even as a child. His adult life was marked by drug abuse, alcoholism, criminality and (as his lawyer argued) religious apathy. This attempted arsonist illustrates a second key feature of violence in God's name: apathy and extremism often go hand in hand.

Every author on religion and violence writes from a vantage point – be it secular or religious. They should aim at a fair description of traditions that differ from theirs. To better understand the logic undergirding killing in God's name, we must shed the belief that 'someone with beliefs similar to my own would never do that'. Even secularism has to reckon with horrors that stretch from Enlightenment anti-Semitism to communist massacres to a recent mass shooting of Christians in Texas.

Religious violence is not something that only people with 'other' beliefs might participate in. Further, 'secular' killing is not necessarily more rational, restrained or humane than 'religious' killing. Whatever tradition we identify with (be it secular or religious), people in the past or present with similar beliefs have perpetrated unspeakable atrocities in the name of those beliefs. The community without sin can cast the first stone.

Readers will benefit most from this Element if they adopt five attitudes: curiosity, self-criticism, humility, empathy and charity. *Curiosity.* Readers should be more curious about killing. Why did perpetrators think their actions were right or righteous? What keeps me from acting like them? Readers should also be curious about those who act on their beliefs in charitable, inspiring and humane ways. *Self-criticism*. Failure to see the plank in our tradition's eye will hinder analysis of the speck in the eye of another tradition. *Humility*. Examining the failures and abuses of the past should foster humility. It should be hard for a Christian, Muslim, Hindu or atheist to be arrogant about their tradition when they are keenly aware of the skeletons in their historical closet. *Empathy*. The more controversial an issue becomes, the more empathy becomes indispensable. Empathy is wrongly treated as synonymous with 'agreement' and 'consent'. Some assume empathy forestalls critique. However, empathy sharpens critique precisely because it helps one better understand other people's ideas and actions (Hochschild 2016: xi). *Charity*. Treat other people's beliefs as you would want them to treat your own.

Individuals, groups and nations seldom take responsibility for the backlash prompted by their ideas, attitudes and actions. Religious people dislike the growing secularism; however, they often fail to recognise that secular dominance responds to the dogmatic, uncompromising, uncharitable and violent elements within their religious tradition. Secular people dislike the religious resurgence of recent years; however, they often fail to recognise that the religious renewal responds to the dogmatic, uncompromising, uncharitable and violent elements within their secular tradition. Both are tempted to view themselves as embattled victims. However, once an individual or group has taken on the identity of a victim (and they often genuinely are), it is difficult for them to see when they victimise others (Enns 2012). The victimhood pendulum only reverses direction. Rather than take responsibility for the backlash, secular and religious actors often view the backlash as a confirmation that their ideas, attitudes and actions were right and righteous. Is there a way out of such self-confirming polarisation? I propose recovering the virtues of curiosity, self-criticism, humility, empathy and charity. Whether secular or religious, individuals and communities are responsible for how they act on their beliefs and traditions.

1.1 The Problem of God and the Problem of No God

This introductory section complicates our understanding of religion, secularism and the justification of killing. Section 2 then overviews five important theories about the relationship between religion and violence. Section 3 argues that there are few risk-free beliefs, illustrating this point from a brief overview of sacred texts and theology. Section 4, the Element's core, argues for a new understanding of how justice and holiness relate in the minds of those engaged in conflict. Section 5 interrogates common misunderstandings about 'extreme' and 'moderate' faith. And a final section overviews how people might better respond to violence perpetrated in the name of God.

Discussing secularism is essential for several reasons. First, less religion is often seen as the alternative to violent religion or as the solution for it. Second, secularism provides an influential lens – perhaps the most prominent one – through which lethal acts are interpreted. Third, to prevent violence and promote reconciliation, the 'problem of no God' should be considered alongside the 'problem of God'.

What is secularism? Some definitions relate to a historical process spanning centuries, a process that changed the nature of faith in Europe, North America and elsewhere. The 'secularisation thesis' or 'modernisation theory' posited a trajectory: religion's role in public life would decline. However, events of the last few decades have led one of its main proponents to declare the thesis 'falsified'. Now there is talk of the 'return of religions', 'desecularisation' or living in a 'post-secular' world (Bessel 2015: 41–2, 57). Whether faith is reviving or never withered away, non-believers and believers need to understand religion better. In *The Secular Bible*, Jacques Berlinerblau argues that 'today's secularists are biblically illiterate'. Religious illiteracy is a 'looming political liability' (2005:1, 4). Even in secular societies, Scripture has 'become lodged in the muscle memory of civilisation' (2005: 141). The 'return of religions' will require non-believers to engage with faith seriously.

Although religion is not retreating, secularisation has profoundly influenced religious communication in pluralistic spaces. Whereas in previous centuries, it was natural and expected for people to speak of transcendent purpose or divine agency, a powerful frame of reference has become more mundane and 'immanent' (Taylor 2007: 270; Wuthnow 2012: 296). Detailed religious talk cuts against the grain of public discourse. I say 'detailed' because many public figures in countries like the United States commonly practice 'generic' talk of the divine (Soper and Fetzer 2018: 50–6).

The shift from detailed to generic God-talk (or no God-talk) influences discussions of violence. Although attributing agency to God in warfare was once normal (Rowley 2024), modern public discourse in Western countries has little room for it. Someone who believes God acted in war may no longer publicly articulate their belief. A century ago, the *New York Times* might have featured warfare sermons; now, they might run an op-ed criticising Christian nationalism.

A significant caveat must be made. In times of shock, stress and danger, religious rhetoric proliferates. The 9/11 terrorist attacks, for example, led to a bipartisan outpouring of public trust in providence. However, politicians (especially those on America's Left) quickly returned to bridled God-talk. As I write this section in late February 2022, a similar shift appears to be occurring due to Russia's invasion of Ukraine. Some in both countries are framing the conflict – between Russia's aggression and Ukraine's resistance – in religious terms. The 2022 invasion sparked a dramatic shift in European policies towards armament, a renewed appreciation for territorial integrity and self-determination and a dramatic change in perceptions about where history is headed. Some have used words like 'holy war', 'righteous cause' and 'moral clarity' to describe Ukraine's armed resistance (e.g. Hamid 2022). Words like 'evil', 'uncivilised' and 'barbaric' are attached to Vladimir Putin. Russian aggression shows how quickly such talk re-emerges within secular societies.

'Secularisation' refers to a controversial theory about historical trajectory. 'Secularism' can have many meanings: a way of regulating public institutions; ideas about policing the use of symbols or spaces in a pluralistic society; a legally enforced foundation for government; or disbelief in the supernatural. Jacques Berlinerblau categorises various secularisms. The first cluster appears under the heading 'non-belief/anti-religion': '(1) atheism; and/or (2) the opposite, or nemesis, of religion; and/or (3) a system that wishes to destroy religion' (Berlinerblau 2022: 2). A second cluster falls under 'political secularism': '(4) a political doctrine for regulating how the state, on the one side, will interact with the church, mosque, synagogue, ashram, what have you, on the other'. 'Non-belief/anti-religion' and 'political secularism' differ, although Soviet secularism was an example of anti-religious political secularism. Some forms of political secularism 'have little to do with nonbelief or dislike of religion' – like India or the United States (5). 'Political secularism', Berlinerblau argues, 'is an idea born of *religious* thinkers contemplating *religious* problems using a *religious* vocabulary to solve them'. The Hebrew Bible, New Testament and patristic and Protestant theologians inadvertently laid the groundwork for political secularism (16; cf. 13–48).

'Secularism' can pair with different attitudes towards nonconformists. Scott Hibbard notes how 'secularism, religion, and nationalism all have their liberal and illiberal variants, and neither religion nor secularism is necessarily hostile to the demands of an inclusive and open society' (2015: 104–5). He differentiates between secularisms. He calls exclusivist and closed forms 'irreligious secular nationalism'. This version is hostile towards competing sources of loyalty, especially religion. It greatly contributes to ideological conflict, particularly when countered by illiberal forms of religion. A second variant, 'ecumenical secular nationalism', aims at neutrality towards religion and even protects 'religion and conscience from political intrusion' while also protecting the rights of religious minorities (107). The ecumenical version, he argues, often slides into anti-religious and intolerant practices. This illiberal turn is evident in claims that any religious expression in the public realm is inherently illegitimate (100–23).

Few convictions are entirely risk-free, immune to abuse or resistant to manipulation; most contain the possibility of leading to unforeseen or unintended consequences. Some scholars link certain religious beliefs with a willingness to take life: deference to sacred texts or religious authority, belief in moral absolutes or belief in future rewards or punishments (see scholarly claims in Rowley 2014). Many believers assert that there *are* texts that communicate truths about God, there *are* ordained hierarchical relationships, some actions *are* right and others wrong and there *is* an afterlife with judgements or rewards. The afterlife raises the stakes for earthly behaviour. If such convictions have been employed when justifying violence, some might respond by negating these claims: There *are no* sacred texts or authority, there *are no* absolute moral rights and wrongs and there *is no* future state with rewards or punishments. Might these negations also be used to justify violence?

Non-religious and anti-religious forms of secularism tend to be marked by negation. Consider an interview with Christopher Hitchens. He was asked about the unconventional views on ending human life as advocated by Princeton's controversial ethicist, Peter Singer. Hitchens replied: 'There's no discipline, there's no faith, there's no [atheist] dogma that means I have to [do what he says], so [Peter Singer] can't legislate for me. . . . [W]e don't have bishops. We don't have priests. We don't have popes' (Taunton 2016: 99). Hitchen defined secularism against the dominant faith tradition (a negation of Christianity). He described a multiplicity of non-theistic moral identities (Singer's ethics are not representative). He also highlighted the relative autonomy of the individual (there is no agreed-upon body of doctrines).

In *Secularisms*, Janet R. Jakobsen and Ann Pellegrini argue that secularism in its dominant Western form grew out of Christianity (mainly Protestantism). 'Secularism' defines itself against what it rejects. Consider Hitchens' words. He could have said atheists lack imams or rabbis (and perhaps he does elsewhere), but he chose Christian examples: bishops, priests, popes. Western anti-religious secularism bears the impress of Christianity, but so does political secularism. Exporting secularism fuelled conflict, as happens with imperial endeavours. However, secularism in each region bears the impress of the dominant religion, leading to differences between secular polities like India, Turkey and the United States. Thus, secularism is diverse, just like religion (Jakobsen and Pellegrini 2008: 12).

Non-religious secularisms share a characteristic: a relative paucity of theological beliefs. Hitchens said: 'there's no faith . . . We don't have priests'. Leading unbelievers describe their beliefs as negation – what they do not believe (Antony 2007: xiii; Pinker 2011: 221; Gray 2018: 2). Having cleared the landscape of sacred texts, dogmas and religious authority, some try to construct a positive vision for human flourishing (e.g. Pinker 2018). Many acknowledge a loss of ultimate meaning, purpose and moral certainty. However, they construct meaning, purpose and ethical norms without transcendent appeals – 'the immanent' option, as Simon Blackburn terms it (2007: 190). They often draw on their own intellectual traditions, and some hold their beliefs with sincerity and great intensity and desire to see their convictions reflected in society. Non-theistic secularism is often the assumed antidote to religious violence and extremism. However, if believing in God sometimes exacerbates conflict, discarding belief in God is not free of risk.

1.2 Meaningless and Meaningful Violence

In the early morning of 12 June 2016, Omar Mateen entered Pulse nightclub in Orlando, Florida, and began shooting. He killed forty-nine people and wounded fifty-three before the police killed him. He admired Islamic terrorists and expressed negative attitudes towards homosexuality (Holzer et al.: 2022: 29–30). His lethal actions were terrifyingly *meaningful*. Killing is full of meaning when the killer infuses it with purpose or significance – often of the religious, racial or political variety. This attack was bursting with meaning lethally discharged against the LGBTQ+ community with the additional aims of promoting Islamic rule, intimidating the government and terrifying the populace.

A year later, on the evening of 1 October 2017, Stephen Paddock was perched in a hotel room as he rained bullets on Las Vegas concertgoers. He killed sixty people and wounded hundreds more before committing suicide. Authorities still struggle to find a motive (Holzer et al.: 2022: 276). His actions exemplify terrifyingly *meaningless* or 'senseless' violence. Killing is repulsively meaningless when the motivation is the thrill of planning for and carrying out an attack or when the killing is done in response to minor offences or for meagre benefits. In these cases, the perpetrator's justifications seem anaemic. The lone wolf terrorist with no apparent motive (Paddock's meaningless killing) terrifies at least as much as the one who clearly articulates repulsive motivations (Mateen's meaningful killing).

Meaning and morality are closely related. Most violence has a prominent moral component (Fiske and Rai 2015: 13). Without denying other 'non-moral motives for violence', it seems 'most violence under most ordinary conditions in all cultures throughout history and prehistory' is morally motivated (301). Humans have a natural sense of morality that informs attitudes towards lethal force. The moral sense is often misguided. Rabbi Jonathan Sacks recently coined the term 'altruistic evil' to describe 'evil committed in a sacred cause, in the name of high ideals'. He argued that 'there is nothing specifically religious about' it (2015: 9–10). The pairing of lethality and morality has led Stephen Pinker to argue that there is 'far too much morality' in the world (2011:751). His position is understandable, given examples where someone's warped morality facilitated injustice. However, religion and morality can also hinder violence. A decreased sense of morality might solve some problems and create others.

This Element focuses on meaningful and self-consciously moral killing, not its meaningless and amoral counterpart. Historically, most killers made robust claims about justice or holiness – and often both. However, meaningful killing comes in different forms. Lethally ushering in a communist utopia is meaningful, as is killing in defence of the innocent. Reclaiming the Holy Land is meaningful, as is an armed revolt against slave-masters. Protecting the fatherland is meaningful, as is targeting an abortion provider. Secular violence may be infused with less meaning, but that does not make it meaningless. Highlighting how all these acts are meaningful does not mean they are morally equivalent – quite the opposite. We can now ask deeper questions about how one's sense of meaning relates to beliefs about justice.

Killing tends to be meaningful because the object is human. Religion furnishes humans with teachings about humanity – what a human is, how they should live, what obligations they owe each other and how to respond when these obligations are violated. Unsurprisingly there is a tight linkage between meaning, religion, views of humanity and the justification of lethal force. Religions help believers differentiate just from unjust lethal or coercive acts. Religion also helps people make sense of chaos and killing, and violence shapes religious belief and practice (Meral 2018: 21). Many religions teach that the divine cannot be indifferent to the killing of any human, be they a foe or friend, a religious outsider or a co-religionist. Taking life is never *meaningless* from the divine perspective.

For those who view humans as sacred, killing humans relates to beliefs about the holy. Timothy Samuel Shah argues that 'violence intrinsically tilts towards unsecularity'. Killing makes 'ultimate issues unavoidable .... Contrary to fashionable thinking, this [pairing of religion and violence] is not so much because religion is naturally violent. Instead, it is because violence is naturally religious' (Shah 2015: 397–8). Whether one is protesting an injustice or perpetrating an atrocity, religion often accompanies the loss of life.

Sacred texts often set the contours for beliefs about humanity and taking human life. 'Whoever takes a life unjustly has committed so tremendous a sin in God's eyes that, as the Qur'ān states, "it is as if he has killed all of humankind"' (Brown 2016: 16). Consider also the earliest command to kill in the Hebrew Bible. Genesis 9:6 grounded capital punishment in the *imago dei* – the doctrine that humanity resembled God. The perpetrator images God (grounding moral responsibility), and the victim images God (accentuating the crime).

The verse sanctions killing an *imago dei* (the perpetrator) because they killed an *imago dei* (the victim). A very high view of humanity undergirded retributive justice (Wilson 2017: 263–73). Both killings – of the victim and then of the perpetrator – are meaningful acts related to God. The Abrahamic faiths call for justice against perpetrators, even as they 'anchor the possibility of forgiveness and reconciliation in God' and 'also emphasize the necessity of extending forgiveness to the neighbor' (Kärkkäinen 2016: 6, 8).

Lethal acts are informed by language (as when Scripture shapes the contours of belief and behaviour), but killing also creates language. Warfare produces language that grapples with meaning (Lepore 1998: x). Whether observing or participating, winning or losing, language helps make sense of the loss of life. Language plays a crucial part in justifying life-taking: justifying it to oneself, to co-belligerents, to enemies or to the watching world. (When we speak of people 'justifying' killing, we do not mean the killing was actually just and therefore justified. The word is a shorthand for 'attempted justification' (Clarke 2014: xi).)

In sum, most killing is meaningful because the perpetrator ascribes meaning to it. Meaning, however, is ambiguous and volatile – promoting unsettling and inspiring behaviour. One's sense of meaning is deeply informed by religion, particularly by sacred texts and their teachings about humanity. Language informs killing and is a product of it. Language helps make sense of bloodshed even as it is used to justify bloodshed. This discussion has been building up to a simple point that is often overlooked in secular societies. Because humans are meaning makers and meaning seekers, because religion and sacred texts help interpret events and because killing demands interpretation, justifying or describing conflict through one's religious worldview is normal. Mere 'this-worldly' accounts of killing are the aberration (Shah 2015: 360–406). Religious interpretations of conflict are the rule, not the exception.

The following discussion aims to complicate two other modern assumptions. Does less religion make humans more restrained? Does the separation of Scripture from politics necessarily lead to less killing? An increase in direct religious influence on the state is not necessarily accompanied by an increase in lethality. As a corollary, we should not assume that the secularisation of laws necessarily reduces lethal force.

1.3 Who Would Trust an Atheist with a Nuclear Weapon?

Religion multiplies reasons; it increases the number of possible beliefs one can hold about killing. By contrast, secular people often have fewer beliefs about war. A non-believer might advocate war on this-world grounds like law, rights, public good or human flourishing. The religious also have this-world arguments, but they often articulate other-world grounds as well. Religious people have a greater storehouse of rationales to draw on. Some religious rationales permit ('thou shalt') and others restrain ('thou shalt not'). A religious person might advocate war ('thou shalt defend the innocent') but try to limit war crimes ('thou shalt not target the innocent').

The multiplication of convictions among the religious is a mixed blessing, as is the relative paucity of theological convictions among the irreligious. However, the discussion is often reductionistic: 'Those who believe X have done Y violence; therefore X belief is dangerous and should be discouraged.' The reality is more complex. We might illustrate the relationship between beliefs and behaviours with a bicycle wheel. The hub is a conviction (e.g. belief in the afterlife). The spokes are the practices that radially protrude from the hub. The spokes point outward, and some go in entirely opposite directions (see Figure 1).

A single believer might have dozens or hundreds of belief hubs (one for eschatology, another for election, another for the uncoerced nature of true faith, etc.). The complex interplay between these belief hubs often influences some-one's attitude towards violence. (For example, a belief hub concerning an imminent apocalypse might make violence attractive. This belief might be mitigated by another belief that Jesus told followers to lay down the sword.)

Consider the vexed relationship between beliefs in the afterlife and the potential use of nuclear weapons. It is commonly argued that belief in the afterlife fosters irrational violence in this present life, precisely because eternal rewards are so alluring. However, convictions about the afterlife can lead to many different attitudes towards killing.

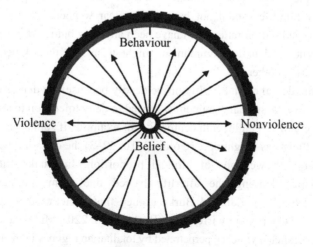

Figure 1 Belief hub

Beliefs in the afterlife foster earthly injustice. Might anticipated heavenly rewards foster earthly irresponsibility? Consider a claim by Yuval Noah Harari in *Homo Deus*: 'people who believe in a heavenly afterlife should not be given nuclear weapons' (2017: 217). His point is powerful because its truth is assumed. Harari characterises belief in the afterlife (the bicycle wheel hub) as having spokes that point in the direction of earthly irresponsibility.

Nuclear weapons are currently strewn across the politico-religious landscape: China, North Korea, Russia, France, India, Israel (presumed), Pakistan, the United Kingdom and the United States. Each nation has a dominant – although not universally shared – way of relating religion and politics. Some of these nations closely link religion and state. Others formally separate religion from politics or establish atheism. It is easy to imagine a situation where religious differences, say between Pakistan and India, might contribute to nuclear war. And to Harari's claim, if such a war erupted, it seems reasonable to assume that beliefs about an afterlife would play some role, along with other political, ethnic, cultural, historical or sociological factors. But what kind of role? Would belief in the afterlife make Muslims or Hindus more or less responsible? For Harari's assertion to be true, he must demonstrate that belief in the afterlife primarily leads towards negative actions on earth, a much-disputed claim (Johnson 2016).

Denial of the afterlife fosters earthly injustice. Harari also seems to suggest that those without belief in a 'heavenly afterlife' might be more responsible with nuclear weapons. However, he coded for the dangers of religion but did not code for the dangers of irreligion (for example, if China or North Korea used their arsenal, few would connect this action with their irreligion). He does not entertain the alternative possibility: 'people who [do not] believe in a heavenly afterlife should not be given nuclear weapons'. Some regimes claiming to be built on rationalism have been anything but restrained, and the millions who died under communism might wish that their killers feared punishment in another life.

Might the denial of an afterlife prove deadly because one denies ultimate accountability? A similar argument was used to deny toleration to atheists in the seventeenth and eighteenth centuries. For example, if John Locke would not trust atheists as neighbours (Goldie 2010: 52–3), he certainly would not trust them with weapons of biblical proportion. In Quaker-influenced Pennsylvania, denying the afterlife barred one from holding office (Maclear 1995: 54). Edmund Burke argued that societies that destroyed religion were destroyed by irreligion (Burke 1790: 220). Many have argued that the unparalleled violence perpetrated by totalitarian regimes in the twentieth century stemmed from the removal of religious restraints (Bessel 2015: 56).

For example, during the Cold War, many in the United States framed the conflict with the nuclear-armed USSR as a struggle against the forces of 'godless communism'. (During the collapse of the USSR, a militantly atheist nation welcomed Orthodox Christianity in the front door and aggressively pursued the rebaptism of the State and a sacralisation of the military. Russia's resurgent religious nationalism is currently a cause for nuclear concern.) The fear of the godless, expressed by Locke and others, might also explain part of why 'secularists remain among the most distrusted groups in the United States' (Baker and Smith 2015: 4). However, a growing body of literature by unbelievers argues that discarding dogma can foster highly ethical societies (Wielenberg 2013: 89–103). Intriguingly, highly irreligious nations are some of the most desirable and least desirable places to live. Some irreligious nations excel at promoting human rights, and others at violating them (Zuckerman 2013: 506).

In the present, there is an ambiguous relationship between political secularism (or state atheism) and violence. French *laïcité* might represent the responsible face of a secular nation in possession of nuclear weapons, but France is by no means the only face. Does the state atheism of nuclear powers like China or North Korea undergird or undermine international stability? North Korea's official state ideology (the atheistic *Juche* that is roughly summarised as 'self-reliance') is conjoined with a military-first (*songun*) approach to national greatness that legitimises political authority by leveraging the possession of nuclear weapons (Smith 2021: 143–4). Does the world rest more secure knowing that Kim Jong-un does not believe in divine judgement? He may have fewer beliefs about the afterlife, but this does not translate into fewer fears about his possession of nuclear weapons. Certainly, if Kim Jong-un believed he would be rewarded in the afterlife, this belief might make him more trigger-happy. However, the threat of eternal punishment could also curb baser instincts.

Beliefs in the afterlife foster earthly restraint. Religious differences between Pakistan and India could lead to nuclear war (given widespread sympathy for terrorists in the former and the growth of Hindu nationalism in the latter). Muslims and Hindus believe in a life after death, and both believe the quality of the afterlife is predicated in some way on actions or beliefs in this life. Both have self-interested reasons to avoid negative consequences after death. They might exercise restraint for deeply personal reasons that are related to the afterlife. Even as future rewards might incentivise killing in some circumstances, fear of future punishment might also restrain. Heaven motivates some Islamists to violent conquest and others to work through the democratic process (Hamid 2016: 9–10).

A recent book, *God Is Watching You*, explored the social effect of belief in an all-seeing God who holds humanity accountable. The fear of divine retribution – in this life or the next – often contributes to remarkably stable societies (Johnson 2016; cf. Wright 2016: 159–83). The desire to avoid retribution can foster restraint towards others – family, neighbours, foreigners or enemies – while incentivising prosocial behaviours like forgiveness and cooperation. Muslims learn in the Qur'an that Allah rewards overlooking offence (Surah 42:40–3). Jews and Christians should forego vengeance precisely because there is a God who acts (Deut. 32:35; Prov. 5:21–2; Rom. 12:17–20). Within Christianity, there is significant theological pressure against using lethal force. John Rawls, a leading theorist of political liberalism, acknowledged that many branches of Christianity set a much higher standard on killing civilians than his own moral theory (1999: 103–5). Those in historic peace churches, like the Mennonites, Society of Friends (Quakers) or the Church of the Brethren, might avoid holding governmental positions that put them in a position to decide on the use of nuclear weapons. And many within the Roman Catholic Church advocate what James Turner Johnson calls 'functional pacifism' (Johnson 2012: 241). These groups possess fundamentally religious restraints on violence.

If we return to our image of a bicycle wheel, with beliefs as the hub and the spokes as the behaviours, the picture looks far more complicated. It is true, as Harari argued, that belief in an afterlife can lead people into bloodshed. However, many other spokes are coming out of the hub, and some point in the opposite direction. Not only that, we have argued that there is also an irreligious bicycle wheel with disbelief in any future state as the hub. Similarly, the spokes project radially from this belief, leading some to eschew violence and others to justify it. Rather than treat religion as unrestrained and irreligion as restrained (or vice versa), taking a more nuanced approach is better. If belief in God facilitates or fuels violence in some circumstances, it proscribes and prevents it in others. Having complicated the relationship between theology and violence, we will now do the same with legislating from sacred texts.

1.4 Who Wants to Live Under a Theocracy?

After a conference in Italy on religion and violence, I asked my dinner companions a question: 'Would you rather live in an English society that had the capital punishment laws of the nineteenth century or in an English society with the "theocratic" capital punishment laws of the Puritans in the seventeenth century?' The answer seemed obvious, especially for the vigorous defenders of secularism at the table: Enlightenment fosters restraint.

Academics express similar sentiments. Consider the account of historical progress in Stephen Pinker's *The Better Angels of Our Nature* (2011):

> In biblical, medieval, and early modern times, scores of trivial affronts and infractions were punishable by death, including sodomy, gossiping, stealing cabbages, picking up sticks on the Sabbath, talking back to parents, and criticizing the royal garden. During the last years of Henry VIII, there were more than ten executions in London *every week*. By 1822 England had 222 capital offenses on the books, including poaching, counterfeiting, robbing a rabbit warren, and cutting down a tree. (180)

Pinker lumps together 'trivial' laws from several centuries without differentiating between those from non-Christian custom, the Hebrew Bible or the whims of capricious kings. He also jumps from Henry VIII (d. 1547) to 1822, skipping over important developments from the Protestant Reformation.

As many critics have argued, Pinker often misunderstands historical trajectory in a book about historical trajectory (the subtitle being *Why Violence Has Declined*). Doubtless, the medieval and early modern periods witnessed executions for 'trivial affronts and infractions', and much of my scholarship emphasises how and why Protestants shed prodigious blood. However, the relationship with sacred texts was far more complicated. To my dinner companions after the conference, I said: 'Although both regimes were far from ideal, the "theocratic" laws of the seventeenth century were more restrained than their more secular counterparts two centuries later.' I explained how *The Massachusetts Body of Liberties* (1641) almost entirely restricted capital punishment to offences listed in the Pentateuch (twelve offences). The Hebrew Bible moderated the treatment of the poor and did not allow capital punishment for crimes like theft (Winship 2019: 166–9). The Puritan emphasis on the rule of God and the law of God led them towards a greater separation of church and state. Pennsylvania Quakers further reduced capital crimes in the 'Great Law' of 1682.

New England Puritans lost power towards the end of the seventeenth century. Their religious 'zealotry' and their reliance on Scripture as a political text became an embarrassment in many quarters. However, unmooring law from the Hebrew Bible did not reduce capital offences. Rather, capital crimes increased tenfold. In England, 'Parliament created myriad new capital offenses in the late seventeenth and eighteenth centuries' (Banner 2002: 7), and many of these laws made their way to New England. As Pinker notes, by '1822 England had 222 capital offenses on the books'. Although Puritan executions would be deemed 'religious violence', nineteenth-century executions for theft would not be attributed to a gradual secularisation. This is another example of scholars coding for religious violence but not coding for violence inflicted during the process of secularisation.

The point of this discussion is not to advocate for scripturally based capital punishment laws. Nor is it to say that Puritan views of capital punishment are ideal. Rather, scholars should not view Scripture-based laws as unrestrained and more secular laws as restrained (or vice versa). Scripture facilitates or fuels violence in some circumstances, and it proscribes and prevents it in others. In the seventeenth century, the application of biblical law reduced the number of capital offences. The subsequent jettisoning of biblical restraints led to a drastic expansion of capital crimes.

The word 'theocracy' conjures ideas of repression, closed-mindedness and violence, with good reason. Yet, the history of the development of religious toleration shows that many proponents of pluralism believed they were more faithful to God's rule than those justifying persecution. For example, Roger Williams' conviction that Christ should rule undergirded his forceful advocacy of universal toleration (Rowley 2017). He strove to bring law into conformity with Scripture precisely because Scripture heightened ethical obligations. In the present, one of the least likely persons to justify killing and coercion, Duke University's distinguished Stanley Hauerwas, is an unashamed theocrat, although his version of the rule of God is a far cry from the vision put forward by other theocrats. In fact, he is a pacifist because he is a theocrat (Hauerwas 2012: 248).

The spectre of 'theocracy' has long been used by secular regimes to justify domination and violence. For the better part of a century, the People's Republic of China has justified the repression of Tibetans, in part, by arguing they were liberating Tibet from the Dalai Lama's theocratic feudalism (Lie and Weng 2020: 140). There are ample grounds to be concerned about Islamists who call for the rule of Allah and the imposition of sharia. However, for many Muslims – especially those living under brutal secular authoritarianism in the Middle East – calls for sharia are made to elevate human dignity, secure rights, limit violence and hold authority accountable. Because these regimes criminalise 'moderate' expressions of faith, it is unsurprising that there is a resurgence of the more 'extreme' movements for building Islamic nations.

As with the above section about the afterlife, the 'rule of God' is another hub on a bicycle wheel with spokes pointing in different directions. In many circumstances, the belief that God must rule can lead to conflict and killing; in other circumstances, it pushes people to articulate robust reasons for living with difference. Similarly, those committed to purging religion from law have an ambiguous relationship with violence. Efforts to restrict religious law have undoubtedly led to reduced violence in many instances and contributed to human flourishing in a pluralist society. However, crusaders against theocracy can tread the same path as medieval crusaders and justify violence against theological outsiders.

1.5 Religion, Secularism and Violence

We have argued that secularism has many similarities to religion, in both its diversity of beliefs and the wide range of practices sanctioned in its name. Secularism can be paired with different ethical norms, political ideologies and visions for human flourishing. One of the characteristics of secularism is a relative lack of beliefs compared to religions. The beliefs of believers can encourage or limit violence. The same is true of the unbelief of unbelievers. Once the secular recognise that their beliefs can be *part* of the problem of conflict, then they can also be *part* of the solution.

In *The Justification of Religious Violence*, Steve Clarke argues that sacred justifications for war function similarly to secular ones, although 'the religious are able to *feed many more premises* into those structures than the non-religious' (italics added). The religious have more beliefs about violence than the non-religious. These additional beliefs can encourage or limit killing (2014: 7–8). Religions provide more reasons to demand justice and more to forgive; more reasons to unite and more to divide; more reasons to submit and more to rebel; more reasons to preserve blood, and more to shed it; more reasons to accept responsibility and more to deflect it; more reasons to separate from the world, and more to conquer it. By contrast, secularism and atheism offer fewer things to fight over but maybe also provide fewer resources for restraining violence.

Although secular killing is far from *meaningless*, it often appeals to less meaning. Whereas an atheist might fight over a besieged homeland, a Hindu might fight to protect a piece of land because it is their home *and because the land has a long association with a particular deity*. Whereas an atheist may consider it a human rights violation to target civilians, a Jewish person might consider this act a violation of human rights *because humanity is made in God's image*. Whereas the atheist might value the peacemaker, the Christian might value them *and trust Jesus' words that peacemakers are sons of God*.

2 Does Religion Cause Violence?

The terrorist attacks of 11 September 2001 profoundly shaped the study of violence in the name of God. In 2010, Jack David Eller said, 'the world is awash with books on religion and violence' (2010: 7). By 2016, Ron E. Hassner said that 'More books have been published on Islam and war since 2001 than in all of human history prior to 2001' (2016: 3). In the wake these terrorist attacks, all religious belief was put in the dock. Nearly every religious group, large and small, and almost every aspect of religious life has been examined for its potential relationship to violence. Religion and theology were treated as an agent – as if they were people flying planes into buildings. Yet it is always humans who choose to act on their beliefs in violent ways. This section overviews five influential theories about religious violence. Before analysing scholarly approaches, we should get a better handle on terminology. Every key term in this Element – 'religion', 'violence' and 'extremism' – is contested.

2.1 Defining Terms

Religion: Any book using the term 'religion' should orient the reader to definitional difficulties (Carlson 2011: 7–22). Religion looks more complicated the more it is examined. James W. Jones notes dozens of definitions of terrorism, and in a class on religion, 'after 15 weeks [of trying to define religion] we had utterly failed at the task .... So arriving at the definition of "religious terrorism" would seem to involve combining the unknown with the obscure' (2008: 3–5). Religion is a vast phenomenon that includes many features of human behaviour, community, history and identity beyond the beliefs that people hold.

Some argue that religion, as a category, is a modern concept (Nongbri 2013), and this etymological argument has important implications for the study of violence. James Bernard Murphy offers a good summary:

> If we cannot agree upon what counts as a religion, then the concept of religion cannot help us to explain violence. Since some kinds of Buddhism and Confucianism make no reference to any god and since Marxism offers a transcendent view of the meaning of history, there seems to be no way to define religion that can exclude Marxism but include Buddhism. The very notion of religion seems to be too imprecise to illuminate or explain anything about violence. (Murphy 2014: 481)

Religion, as I use the problematic but inescapable term, relates to ideas, actions or faith assumptions about the transcendent, the sacred or the holy.

Violence: The term 'violence' is equally divisive. Who or what can be the agents of violence: people militaries, systems, institutions, laws or language? What constitutes a violent act: legitimate physical force, illegitimate physical force, verbal assault, emotional manipulation, social expectations, religious strictures, unkind words or unconscious bias? Does intent matter when deciding if something is violent? Who decides when something is or is not harmful, abusive or violent: the perpetrator, the state, a religious authority, a sacred text, the victim or society? How do we differentiate between concepts like violence, force, power, pressure or coercion? Also, some might question whether 'killing' should be used instead of 'violence' because people generally do not refer to their lethal acts as violence.

'Violence' is something 'they' do. The term generally implies that a lethal act is *unjust*, and thus definitions of violence are intertwined with competing ideas of justice.

Definitions are often rooted in prejudice – in how one *pre-judged* the justice of an act. Thus, what deserves the label of 'violence' often closely corresponds with one's prior religious or political commitments. *Who* or *what* can be the object of violence: the environment (Glazebrook 2001: 322–43), animals (Achoulias 2016: 84–113), a foetus (Ingersoll 2013: 315–23)? This final example is perhaps the most controversial. Many pro-life people across several religions believe that intentionally ending life in the womb *violates* sacred rights. A small fraction believes countering abortion with violence is acceptable or laudable (just as only a small fraction of pro-choice activists praise the recent spate of firebombings at pro-life facilities in 2022). Is abortion violence or is ending the life of abortion providers violence? Mark Juergensmeyer's seminal analysis of abortion-doctor killers presupposes that abortion is not violent (2000: 20–30), but he does not argue for this restricted definition. Similarly, Stephen Pinker does not believe abortion constitutes violence, but he frankly acknowledges what is at stake in the semantic debate: 'If abortion counts as a form of violence, the West has made no progress in the treatment of children. ... [T]he moral state of the West hasn't improved; it has collapsed' (2011: 514). Counting the foetus as an object of violence challenges Pinker's thesis that violence has markedly declined since the Enlightenment (even though statistics on historical abortions are scant). This discussion of abortion exemplifies what is at stake, on both sides, in how one uses terms.

Definitions of 'violence' range from narrow to broad (Bessel 2015: 11–16). When narrowly defined, violence refers to physical bodily injury that sometimes results in death. Narrow definitions tend to be more *objective*, meaning one can count dead bodies or measure wounds. Scholars who employ narrow definitions would not deny other types of harm, but they think there are analytical and legal benefits to reserving 'violence' for certain acts (Clarke 2014: 8–10). In contrast, broad definitions tend to be more *subjective*. Action, as well as the failure to act, can be violent (e.g. 'silence = violence'). There are also many types of violence, encompassing the psychological, spiritual, legal, systemic, economic, linguistic and emotional – and sometimes the harm is not physical. A narrow definition might include the corporal punishment of an infidel but exclude how a legal system might make it more difficult for a religious minority to gain a good education. A broad definition might consider both violence.

Definitional clarity is further complicated by modern linguistic trends related to terms like violence, harm, aggression and abuse. Recent studies on 'micro-aggression' have emphasised the seemingly insignificant ways one can, intentionally or unintentionally, harm another (Sue 2010). A far greater number of actions are termed 'harmful' or 'violent', and the bar has been significantly lowered for when an act becomes violent. This expansion has been called 'concept creep' (Haslam 2016: 1–17). These combined changes have contributed to the proliferation of accusations of harm, violence and abuse. Past actions that might not have been considered harmful – a millennia, a century, a decade, or even a year ago – are now sufficient to make one a pariah, especially on social media.

Increased sensitivity to what constitutes 'harm' is generally a good thing; however, scholars of lethal force often push against overly broad definitions of 'violence' (Juergensmeyer, Kitts, and Jerryson 2013: 3). As the definition expands, violence becomes more subjective (Bessel 2015: 12). The idea of violence becomes less concrete and is less subject to criminal enforcement. Thus, subjective definitions of violence make building consensus around harmful acts harder.

There is a further concern. When society broadens the idea of what constitutes violence and multiplies accusations of violence, apathy towards claims of violence follows. A similar phenomenon has been observed with the accusation that someone is Hitler. The frequent charge that opponents are the Fürher has 'given rise to Hitler fatigue' whereby people doubt that the one dubbed hitlerian is actually dangerous (Rosenfeld 2018). Calling someone 'Hitler' is meant to highlight how dangerous they are, but it often triggers indifference.

Although I recognise many ways to cause harm, and only some leave a physical mark, I generally restrict the term. An example of a narrow definition comes from John D. Carlson, who provisionally defines violence 'as *physical force, often vehement or excessive, used to inflict injury or damage*' (2011: 15; cf. Clarke 2014: 8).

Extremism: This final term is also contested. Many dictionaries list 'moderation' as its antonym. Doubtless, this is often true. However, both moderation and extremism are double-edged. For example, one could argue for a moderate approach towards the 'other' that respects their rights, dignity and self-determination. However, ideas of 'moderation' (Shagan 2011) and 'civility' (Thomas 2018) were often used to dominate subjects or justify imperialism.

'Moderation' can be used to justify or restrict violence; the same is true of 'extremism'. Extremism carries the idea of excess, and usually an excess of zeal, certitude or self-righteousness. Fervently held beliefs can and do fuel acts of injustice. Does religion become extreme the moment it becomes violent? Could someone be an extremist for a just cause? Or does the mixture of lethal force and religious zealotry automatically make the killing unjust? Those deemed religious extremists often have deeply religious reasons for restricting lethal force. Further, apathetic or religiously illiterate believers (in contrast to fervent ones) are often easily swept up in campaigns of xenophobic nationalism. When radicalism and apathy merge, religious history and symbols are drained of much of their theological content.

2.2 Religion Primarily Foments Violence

This section focuses on five theories about the relationship between religion and violence: Religion foments violence; religious violence involves projection; religious violence is a myth; religion restrains violence; religion and violence are ambivalently related. After the terrorist attacks of 9/11, a slew of authors, politicians and pundits argued that religion was especially prone to violence. Some asserted that '[R]eligions are *intrinsically* hostile to one another' (Harris 2004: 225). Because religion is based on what is unprovable, invisible and irrational, believers are unhinged (Avalos 2005). The New Atheists became figureheads for such critiques. Religion was an intellectual virus or mind parasite that destroyed society (Dawkins 2006), a nefarious spell that deluded the masses (Dennett 2006), a poison that ruined everything (Hitchens 2007). Other critics narrow their scope and argue a particular type of religion fosters violence, like traditions with warfare in their sacred texts (Young 2008), fundamentalism (Ellens 2004) or monotheism (Schwartz 1997).

If the problem is religion (or a particular form of it), what is the cure? Some secular authors demand absolute surrender. For the sake of peace, religion must be disarmed. Heretical ideas must burn, one mind at a time. In *Fighting Words*, Hector Avalos excluded most of humanity from peacemaking: 'Involving religion in decision making is never a good idea if the goal is to eliminate or at least minimise violence' (Avalos 2005: 343). The secular minority will issue faithless fiats for the religious majority. For the sake of peace, he wishes to 'eliminate religion from human life altogether' (371). These are fighting words. Jacques D. Berlinerblau, writing from within secularism, argues that such approaches to religion are regressive, unrealistic and intellectually unimaginative (2005: 1–9, 130–41; cf. Pinker 2011: 819).

New Atheist critiques are often accurate and incisive. However, they and their followers have become like what they detest (Teehan 2010: 198–201), a recurring theme in the history of conflict. They are not neutral arbiters of religious conflict but ideological participants in it. They often pour petrol, not water, on the fire. Fantasising about a religion-free society is counterproductive. For example, some scholars argue that because religion is a useful evolutionary adaptation (177–9) – on both the individual and societal level – atheism 'is a battle not just against culture, but against nature' (Johnson 2016: 11). Eradicating religion would thus be *unnatural*.

In *The Fundamentalist Mindset*, Charles B. Stozier and David M. Terman argue that fundamentalism comes in secular and religious forms and fundamentalism is only sometimes directly linked with violence (2010: 3–15; cf. Shah 2015: 360–406). Similarly, J. M. Berger has argued that any ideology, race, religion or nation can take an extremist stance towards out-group members (2018: 4). Some dub the New Atheists as new fundamentalists. They semantically dehumanise the religious, using words like 'virus', 'parasite' and 'poison' to describe religious ideas and those who hold them. Some fantasise about eradicating religious violence by eradicating religion (rightly Teehan 2010: 199). This approach echoes earlier ages when people sought to solve religious problems by removing problematic religions. Karen Armstrong has argued that Richard Dawkins has a 'dangerously' simplistic understanding of religion, secularism and violence (2014: 313), and John Teehan refers to the New Atheists as 'secular extremists' (2010: 199). Armstrong has even argued that 'modern society has made a scapegoat of faith' (2014: 1). This is a pointed critique because René Girard's theory asserts that those scapegoating remain *unenlightened* – driving into the wilderness one who was not to blame for societal woes (Girard 1986).

This religion-foments-violence position also misunderstands the development of modern values. Sam Harris states that 'It is time we acknowledge that no real foundation exists within the canons of Christianity, Islam, Judaism, or any of our other faiths for religious tolerance and religious diversity'. He advocates pursuing peace through 'dispens[ing] with the dogma of faith' (Harris 2004: 225). His account of the origin of modern values is as sweeping as it is uninformed. Scholars note the Christian roots of modern values like human rights and humanitarianism (e.g. Buc 2015: 6–7; cf. Bessel 2015: 55; Berlinerblau 2022: 13–48). Many of these 'modern' values have deeper roots in the Hebrew Bible and find corollaries in Islam and other faith traditions. Further, there is good reason to question whether 'secularism' alone is suited to countering killing in God's name – never mind formulating a universally binding argument that any lethal act *should not have taken place* (Sacks 2015: 5, 256–7).

Blaming religion also allows some non-religious people to ignore their tradition's role in creating and sustaining conflict. Secularisation, globalisation and modernisation – sometimes spread through colonialism – greatly contributed to the instability of the modern world (Armstrong 2014: 286–7). Thus, imagining that the miracle elixir will come from more secularism is hard. Janet Jakobsen, for example, reluctantly arrived at the conclusion that secularism was more violent than religion (Jakobsen 2004; Jakobsen and Pellegrinip 2008; cf. Mason 2015; Shah, 2015: 360–406). Further, a recent analysis of the New Atheists shows their remarkable willingness to justify killing or advocate war through appeals to atheism (Foster, Megoran and Dunn 2017). Jack David Eller rightly notes that if Sam Harris' dream came true and religion ceased, '*violence would not cease to exist*' (Eller 2010: 331; cf. Gopin 2002: 58–9).

How do non-believers respond to the bloodshed enacted by those with similar metaphysical beliefs? Like the religious, some are ignorant of their history or ignore inconvenient episodes (rightly Stark and Corcoran 2014: 65–6). Some acknowledge the abuse but detach it from beliefs about the non-existence of God. And others recognise failure and call for humility and self-criticism. The first is akin to the Christian who idealises Christian history while omitting (or being ignorant of) the Crusades, witch trials or conflict in Northern Ireland. Walter Sinnott-Armstrong and Stephen Pinker illustrate the second approach: acknowledgement with detachment. In an article arguing for why Christianity must be held morally responsible for crimes done in its name, Sinnott-Armstrong offers a brief comment on atheist violence: 'Of course, atheists kill, too. Russian and Chinese communist governments are famous examples. However, these atheists killed in the name of communism, not atheism' (2007: 76). Similarly, Stephen Pinker challenges the notion that the twentieth century was the most violent ever. He argues that the atheistic nature of communist violence is 'irrelevant' because harmful ideas were borrowed from the Bible (2011: 228–41, 818; cf. Avalos 2005: 301–43). These authors claim that such justifications for violence do not flow out of atheist principles per se but from the transformation of atheism into a dangerous religious ideology. Atheism remains an essentially benign force. Wherever atheists are violent, this is not atheist violence (an example of the 'no true Scotsman' fallacy).

Jacques Berlinerblau illustrates the third approach. He argues for an intellectually robust secularism that is rooted in relentless self-critique. The unflattering parts of secular history should be squarely faced:

> The massive and inexcusable human right's failures of polities such as Algeria, Tunisia, North Korea, and the ex-Soviet Union, among others, should be thought about carefully. Indeed, an autopsy of failed secular regimes, particularly those in the Middle East, will be especially useful in conceptualizing the inhumane possibilities that lurk within worldviews that purport to be deeply concerned about humanity. (2005: 136)

He is willing to explore how harmful behaviour grows out of beliefs associated with his own.

2.3 Religious Violence as Projection

A second approach to religion and violence is related to the argument that religion foments violence. Projection involves attributing interior characteristics to something external. An individual or group's desires, fears, hopes and frustrations become externalised. The authors of sacred texts projected their desire to hear from God, or their hope for divine involvement, onto the divine – attributing their violent desires to God. This approach builds on a long history of biblical higher criticism and contextualising sacred texts in the world of the ancient Near East. Some scholars of violence argue that lethal accounts in sacred texts are historically fictitious (Pinker 2011: 10; Eisen, 2011: 26–7, 53; Ward 2006: 112–13). Hebrew Bible conquests, for example, were primarily a literary 'genocide' (Leadbetter 1999: 273), a position that some early Church theologians also embraced. These accounts come from the human mind, not God's. Humans crafted God in their own violent image (Hitchens 2007: 107).

In Europe and the United States, these charges of 'projection' are often primarily aimed at the Jewish and Christian Scriptures. They are secondarily levelled at the Qur'an and other sacred texts. One could even suggest that the New Atheists projected (irony intended) their disgust over Islamic terrorism onto an enemy that it was more socially acceptable to demonise – Christianity. In Western societies, the costs for directly critiquing Islam are often much higher than for critiquing Christianity (Stark and Corcoran 2014: 9–10) because a critic of Islam can be called Islamophobic or racist (Gagné 2016). Even though terms like Christianophobia exist, the label is not widely used and may even be worn as a badge of honour.

If the first form of projection asks how violent narratives made their way into a sacred canon, a second form asks how believers in the present came to think their violence pleased the divine. In this interpretation, those invoking God to justify violence are revealing personal desires, not anything true about God. The human will to power is mistaken for the divine will. Thus, religion is prone to violence because it is a 'fantasy system' that projects individual desires on God – a move that 'renders every act in "his" name irrefutably righteous' (Piven 2004: 120). Scriptural extremists killed based on a fantasy, and modern ones follow suit.

Both claims about projection challenge violent religion by undermining sacred texts. If Joshua did not really kill Canaanites, modern actors should stop appropriating his example. This approach also distances God from acts of violence, past and present. There are also drawbacks to this violence-reduction strategy because it often requires a radical reinterpretation of sacred texts (Bergmann, Murray, and Rea 2011: 1–19), texts that form a core part of individual or collective identity.

Many are unlikely to adopt such changes, especially not believers who might already find violence attractive or necessary. Believers may not listen to critical exegesis precisely because those who offer such critiques throw out much of the scriptural canon. It is also possible that liberal approaches to sacred texts may even confirm the very beliefs they aim to counter: namely, that elites destroy sacred texts to sanitise them. Religious militants, then, can more easily claim the mantle of following the plain reading of the text.

2.4 Religious Violence Is a Myth

William Cavanaugh makes an original and controversial claim about religion and violence. He disrupts many of the above-mentioned arguments by challenging those who believe a transcultural and transhistorical phenomenon called 'religion' is especially prone to violence. 'Religious violence' is a 'myth' in two ways. First, it does not exist. Second, the myth about its existence is a meaning-granting narrative that justifies violence.

First, 'religious violence' does not exist because 'religion' is a problematic term with a violent history. For 'religion' to be a coherent category, the individual 'religions' must bear a family resemblance (as in the natural world, all the *species* bear a resemblance to an overarching *genus*). Although Cavanaugh's critics often accuse him of denying that violence stems from faith commitments, his argument is more nuanced:

> I have no doubt that ideologies and practices of all kinds – including . . . Islam and Christianity – can and do promote violence under certain conditions. What I challenge as incoherent is that there is something called religion – a genus of which Christianity, Islam, Hinduism, and so on are species – which is necessarily more inclined towards violence than are ideologies and institutions that are identified as secular. (Cavanaugh 2009: 5)

Belief in a divine person or persons is a frequently claimed overarching feature (the genus), but this criteria does not fit several so-called religions. Cavanaugh comments on one author's attempted definition: 'His dilemma is this: if he defines religion too narrowly, it will exclude things he wants to include, like Confucianism; if he defines religion too broadly, it will include things he wants to exclude, like Marxism' (Cavanaugh 2009: 20–1). Cavanaugh's book explores that repeated word: 'want'. Definitions accord with people's *desires* as they legitimise power and sanctify bloodshed. Irreligious groups often feature the defining marks of dangerous religion: 'so-called secular ideologies and institutions like nationalism and liberalism can be just as absolutist, divisive, and irrational as those called religious' (Cavanaugh 2009: 10). As such, they are just as prone to violence.

Second, 'religious violence' is a myth because rehearsing this myth grants meaning, authority and legitimacy to the secular state and its violence. The relatively modern dichotomy between 'religious' and 'secular' emerged from power struggles. The ascendant 'secular' order then subordinated religion because it was divisive.

> The myth of religious violence helps to construct and marginalize a religious Other, prone to fanaticism, to contrast with the rational, peace-making, subjects. This myth may be and is used in domestic politics to legitimate the marginalization of certain types of practices and groups labeled religious, while underwriting the nation-state's monopoly on its citizen's willingness to sacrifice and kill. In foreign policy, the myth of religious violence serves to cast nonsecular social orders, especially Muslim societies, in the role of villain. *They* have not yet learned to remove the dangerous influence of religion from political life. *Their* violence is therefore irrational and fanatical. *Our* violence, being secular, is rational, peace making, and sometimes regrettably necessary to contain *their* violence. We find ourselves obliged to bomb them into liberal democracy. (Cavanaugh 2009: 4)

Western societies peddle myths about the dangers of religion to distract from the gravity of violence done in the name of secular values, covering the bodies under a pall of 'restraint' and 'moderation'.

Cavanaugh's thesis helpfully challenges those who simplistically blame religion as the primary cause of violence. Ephraim Radner has interacted with the thesis at length. Radner, like Cavanaugh, is critical of killing in God's name and of the illiberal turn of the liberal state, and both want to see Christianity as a force for good. Although Cavanaugh rightly argues that there are many causal factors (like politics) behind the 'religious wars', Radner emphasises how these wars had distinctly religious characteristics. He continues to use the term 'religious violence', partly because partisans self-identify as motivated by religion. Even though the term 'religion' has a violent history and definitions are unsatisfactory, Radner worries that Cavanaugh's thesis undermines clear-eyed analysis of the role of faith in perpetrating and justifying unspeakable acts. Radner also pushes back on Cavanaugh's argument that an intolerant secular order demonised religion in the name of safety and stability. He argues that deeply religious people in early modern Europe appealed to the state for help in creating institutions that prevented religious differences from devolving into violence (Radner 2012: 1–55).

2.5 Religion Primarily Prevents Violence

Religion might be likened to an apple. For some, 'religious' and 'rotten' are synonyms. When a movement, institution or idea turns absolutist, irrational or extreme, some attach the term 'religion' to it. It is not a compliment to be called religious in this sense. However healthy the apple may appear, the core is rotten. Violence reveals rotten principles at the core. Others insist that religion and faith are fundamentally beneficent. Although there may be spots on the apple, the fruit is fundamentally good. When religion harms, the apple is poisoned. Those who view religion as especially prone to violence (rotten to the core) and those who say true religion is peaceful (wholesome to the core) run the risk of essentialising religion by streamlining a complex phenomenon (Carlson 2011: 10–11).

There are crude and nuanced ways of arguing that true religion is beneficent. In its crude form, people speak of religion in general – or a specific religious tradition – as if it were an overwhelming force for good. Those who approach religious history this way emphasise the good that religion does. However, they often downplay or ignore the evil and claim that evil actors use religion as a mere 'cloak'. When they acknowledge crimes done in the name of their faith, the perpetrators are not 'true' believers (another example of the 'no true Scotsman' fallacy). 'If true religious faith is non-violent', writes Richard Bessel in his summary of this position, 'violence cannot be legitimately justified in the name of religion' (2015: 43). Crusaders were not true Christians, the 9/11 terrorists were not true Muslims and Buddhist nationalist in Sri Lanka were not true Buddhists. People taking this stance often fail to see how violence and extremism can grow out of their belief system. They have difficulty seeing how people with similar faith commitments can arrive at widely divergent attitudes towards violence. This approach also risks not taking perpetrators at their word, namely that perpetrators view themselves as 'true' members of the faith community.

Other scholars are more nuanced and do not believe there is a unique connection between religion and violence. Keith Ward argues that religion sometimes causes harm, but the good outweighs the bad. 'All human beings, religious or not, are prone to evil' (Ward 2006: 42). He defends this point in a chapter entitled 'the corruptibility of all things human'. Charles Kimball's *When Religion Becomes Evil: Five Warning Signs* aims to help readers with 'Distinguishing between corrupt forms of religious expression and authentic, life-affirming forms' (Kimball 2009: 8). Loving and 'authentic' religion is capaciously humane. Evil done in the name of religion result from deviation.

Another nuanced approach that distances religion from violence holds great promise. It is well suited for understanding when and why religions turn harmful. It also helps the religious emphasise the more pacific and tolerant elements in their faith. Miroslav Volf argues that the major religious traditions 'are compelling visions of flourishing'. Of his faith, Christianity, he says 'an authentic faith is always engaged, at work to relieve personal suffering as well as to push against social injustice, political violence, and environmental degradation' (2015: xi, 9). He contends that Christians militarise when they water doctrine down: 'Whenever violence was perpetrated in the name of the cross, the cross was depleted of its "thick" meaning within the larger story of Jesus Christ and "thinned" down to a symbol of religious belonging and power' (Volf 2008: 13). There is something superficial about harmful expressions of Christianity. Sociologist David Martin has made similar arguments when describing the morphing of theology. When the church and state united in violence, the meaning behind Christian logic, symbolism and metaphor was redeployed: 'The symbolic logic of Christianity [was] transformed under social pressure' (Martin 1997: 155; cf. 133–60).

2.6 Religion and Violence Are Ambivalently Related

R. Scott Appleby argues that the sacred is ambivalently related to violence. The sacred itself is not ambivalent; only the imperfect human response to it, leading some towards violence and others towards peace (2000: 30). He pushes against simplistic accounts of religious violence:

> The either/or method of analyzing religion – built on the assumption that one must decide whether religion is essentially a creative and 'civilizing' force or a destructive and inhumane specter from a benighted past – is no less prevalent for being patently absurd. Both positions on religion smack of reductionism. (Appleby 2000: 10)

Sometimes religion legitimises violence, at other times it limits it. This 'deep tension' exists within most faith communities (Appleby 2000: 10–11). Across creeds and centuries, religious actors have done great harm. However, there are also 'religious militants' whose 'sacred rage' is put in the service of ending conflict, pursuing justice and fostering reconciliation (Appleby 2000: 6–13). Religious militants can go to the 'extremes' of sanctifying violence or resisting it (Appleby 2000: 11).

The human response to the sacred, then, is part of the problem and part of the solution. Religious people can enact their faith in ways that inflame conflict or ameliorate it. The task, then, is to understand 'why some people acting in sincere response to the sacred – acting religiously – choose violence over nonviolence, death over life' (Appleby 2000: 27). Appleby's approach aligns closely with that taken in this Element.

3 How Might Theology and Sacred Texts Justify Violence?

I live in an eighteenth-century home and sometimes have questions about repairing it. There is a Facebook group for people like me. Participants ask questions, share historical facts and proudly attach 'before and after' pictures.

Most conversations are cordial. Every few months, seething animosity erupts. There are 'Purists' who believe all renovation must be authentic. 'Pragmatists' argue that purity is too expensive, leading people to abandon historic homes or knock them down. 'Presentists' believe each generation adds to the history by modifying the house. Sometimes the discussion board erupts, usually after a 'Pragmatist' posts a picture of a cost-effective but inauthentic renovation or a 'Presentist' posts about how a historic home was updated to reflect modern tastes. 'Purists' respond, accusing people of 'destroying history' or contributing to 'national decline'. They argue that modern homeowners are decadent and selfish, precisely because they believe they 'own' their home (rather than 'preserve' it). At other times, users post pictures of a newly demolished home and then accuse 'Purists' of raising the standards so high that people are deterred from owning an old home. 'Peacemakers' try to outline the benefits and drawbacks of each approach. All sides share a common belief: historic homes are valuable and should be preserved. The similarities fuel the differences. In this conflict, there is dichotomising between good and evil, beliefs about purity and transgression, invocations of a fabled history, scapegoating and catastrophising. In stern defiance of Godwin's Law, users do not (yet) accuse each other of being like Hitler.

Humans can fight over anything and they will grasp at whatever resources might aid the struggle. Religion, unsurprisingly, is readily at hand. There are many 'religions' (e.g. Judaism, Bahá'í, Mormonism) that are themselves internally pluralistic (e.g. Islam is not only divided between Sunni and Shia, there are subdivisions that include schools of thought like Sufism and Wahhabism). Diversity across time and place adds additional layers of complexity. This section has a daunting task: to overview the content of various beliefs and how these beliefs might relate to violence. Each tradition, and many of the subgroups within each tradition, are the subject of extensive scholarly literature, and the following overview is necessarily cursory.

This section contains many generalisations, and I recognise that variations exist across time and space as to what co-religionists believe and how they act on those beliefs. For example, where the text reads 'Muslims believe', this statement is shorthand for 'many Muslims across the centuries broadly agree that the following is a teaching of the Qur'an'. One should not attribute the most violent expression of Islam to all modern Muslims or project modern extremism onto all eras and aspects of Islamic history (Akyol 2011). In overviewing various traditions, there is the temptation to emphasise differences. The temptation also exists on the other side: to assume that Islam is identical to other religions and has the same resources for war or the same pathway to peace (Hamid 2016). Similar qualifications apply to other faith traditions.

One of the arguments of this Element is that there are few risk-free beliefs. Moral absolutism and the denial of absolutes each solve some problems and create others. Positing heavenly rewards and denying their possibility can each foment or restrict killing. Belief in sacred texts and the denial of sacred texts can each license or limit violence. Believing religion stands above government can be just as dangerous as placing the state above the demands of faith. The ways complex beliefs are held can be as important as the beliefs themselves.

If certain clusters of beliefs have proved fertile ground for the justification of violence, it is important to remember that it is often only a minority who use those beliefs for violent ends. That said, the wider nation or religious community might sympathise with the violence, tolerate it or turn a blind eye towards a perpetrator's actions. Thus, there is often a complex relationship between those who harm and the wider community they belong to. There is also a complex relationship between belief and action. It is often easier to analyse alarming actions than alarming beliefs precisely because the impact of actions is so tangible.

3.1 The Many Causes of Violence

Before overviewing specific religious beliefs, we will explore the vexed issue of causality (see claims about causality in Rowley 2014). Because 'Scholars have identified the roots of religious violence in nearly every aspect of human life' (Burns 2008: 34), the threshold for determining the 'religious' nature of violence is sometimes very low – so low that 'religion' can lose its explanatory force as the cause of violence. After listing commonly claimed factors influencing violence, Lorne L. Dawson writes that 'the mere presence of the factors need not result in violence. In fact, in most instances it will not. A violent outcome is contingent on a complex set of interactions between these internal factors' (2006: 4). I agree.

Because the causes of violence are wide-ranging, the observer has ample opportunity to fall into the trap of confirmation bias. A researcher searching for a link between apocalypticism and violence will find abundant evidence. Psychologists will find cognitive mechanisms at play. Economists will find financial incentives too. Scholars of charismatic personalities will have no shortage of fascinating people to analyse. The error comes not in finding these factors but in placing too much weight on individual elements while overlooking others (Gopin 2002: 4). Violence in God's name is complex, and oversimplification further jeopardises peace because it obscures many causal factors.

This section focuses on the relationship between theological beliefs, sacred texts and the justification of violence. Almost any belief can be weaponised, and religions are storehouses of complex and interrelated beliefs. Even marginal doctrines can be elevated to 'core' identifiers of an 'in-group' and 'out-group'. In these cases, the doctrine itself might not be related to violence; its harmful potential stems from the uses to which the marginal doctrine is put.

At other times, it is the context in which a belief is articulated that makes the belief potentially dangerous. For example, Christians are called to give glory to God in daily life (e.g. Ps. 115:1; Col. 3:17). War is, regrettably, part of life for some. Before, during and after most battles involving Christians, some glorified God for the outcome. What if participation in a particular war, or conduct in that war, was unjust by the standards of the faith? In this case, the believer might praise God for an ungodly act.

3.2 Creation

Beliefs about violence are intimately related to views of human nature, and both beliefs are intertwined with convictions about how the natural order came to be. Religious traditions have approached the topic in divergent ways. In the ancient Near East, the act of creation involved conflict and dismemberment, placing violence at the heart of existence (Holland 2009: 31–2). Similarly, Hindu texts place sacrifice and dismemberment at the beginning of the natural order, and various parts of the sacrificed body are formed into the caste system (Das 2013: 20). In both views, killing is, in some sense, fundamental to nature. Judaism, by contrast, describes creation as an act of the divine will that involved delight ('it was good'), not destruction (Gen. 1–2). Christianity embraces this worldview. Similarly, Islam emphasises creation by divine fiat (Rahman 2009: 65). Thus, the Abrahamic faiths view killing as an aberration from the original creation. They also date the entrance of evil in the world to the creation of humans (or other supernatural beings) who are endowed with some measure of volition.

3.3 The Number of Divine Beings

The quantity of divine beings is important when accounting for violence. This Element has already noted how the 'problem of God' and the 'problem of no God' are related. Additionally, we should consider the 'problem of gods'. It is commonly argued that monotheism is violent because it is exclusivist (Avalos 2005; Schwartz 1997), and polytheism is tolerant because it allows for pluralism. However, polytheistic violence stretches from antiquity into modernity (Meral 2018: 7–8). Polytheism was dominant in the ancient Near East and the Greco-Roman tradition, and these gods were often at war amongst themselves. The gods did not agree on standards of justice or on when killing was appropriate. Thus, it is difficult to ground universally binding ethics in the very gods who are themselves contending for supremacy. Henotheism recognises many gods, but adherents are devoted to one god among many. They worship and obey this god, even though other options are available. Monotheism grounds beliefs about killing in the will and revelation of a single supreme being (even as many religions recognise lesser supernatural beings). God becomes the ultimate standard of justice, and sacred texts often become an indispensable medium for understanding how the divine will relates to conflict situations. Whereas polytheism has trouble grounding universally binding ethics, monotheism tends to push adherents towards a dichotomist view of the world and an exclusivist view of right living. Both positions have important implications for conflict and violence.

3.4 The Nature of Divine Beings

What are the gods or God like? In polytheism, although the gods tend to be described in complex ways, they often specialise in certain activities, like war (e.g. Mars, Athena). In Hinduism, gods like Shiva are associated with destruction. Although Vishnu is often associated with salvation, a future avatar will preside over a cosmic purging involving fire and sword. Many in the Hindu pantheon appear on weaponry across the centuries (LaRocca 1996: 3–12). Deities in Buddhism similarly provide images for war and peace. As Michael Jerryson details, the 'Buddhist pantheon contains violent depictions of deities, bodhisattvas, and spirits' (2013: 58).

In the Hebrew Bible, YHWH has many character-revealing names, and these relate to his might, providential care, jealous love and tender shepherding of his people. He is a God of peace but also of war. He acts as a campaigning general who wins victories for his people, sometimes without any human agency in the struggle (e.g. Exod. 14:14). Christianity adopts this complex portrait of YHWH but argues that there are three persons to this unified God-head. Of particular importance is the person of Jesus, the second member of the Trinity. His Sermon on the Mount puts significant pressure on Christians to forgive and love enemies, and his willingness to die was a testament to these teachings. Christ is also described as a warrior in the eschatological literature of Revelation, and thus Christians can find in Christ both pacific and militant images. The Qur'an's portrait of Allah is similarly multisided. He is described as the majestic, merciful and forgiving creator and sustainer of all things (Rahman 2009: 1–16) but also as a judge, an avenger and a partisan in the conflicts of his people.

3.5 Sacred Texts and Tradition

Scriptures not only make claims about the nature of the gods or God, they are also storehouses of commands ('thou shalt'), proscriptions ('thou shalt not'), historical precedents (as in Islam's Battle of Badr), ways of structuring societies (as in Hinduism's caste system), ways of talking about conflict (as in Christianity's spiritual warfare) and so much more. Sacred texts shape religious language for a given community, fostering continuity in belief and practice across the centuries.

Identifying a sacred corpus can be difficult. For example, outside observers who studied comparative religion during global Western expansion partly constructed the idea of a unified Hinduism built around a fixed set of sacred texts (Das 2013: 15–16). Sometimes there is an agreed-upon collection of texts (like the Qur'an) supplemented by authoritative tradition (the Hadith). Judaism likewise has core texts that form the Hebrew Bible as well as centuries of reflection on these texts and important collections like the Talmud and Mishna. Christians disagree about which texts are canonical (e.g. debates about the Apocrypha) and about the relationship between the Hebrew Bible and the Christian Scriptures. There is also disagreement about the importance of texts following the closing of the canon. Broadly speaking, Orthodox political theology places special weight on the early church fathers and Roman Catholicism on the accumulation of authoritative teachings across the centuries. Protestants deny that any post-biblical texts are indisputably authoritative, even as Protestantism is characterised by written creeds and confessions. The Bahá'í have tens of thousands of sacred texts (Stockman 2020: 1). In the Sikh tradition, the martial and religious swords cohere and the sixth Guru Hargobind (1595–644) embraced arms in self-defence. The final human Guru, Gobind Singh (1666–708), transferred spiritual authority to sacred writ, transforming words into a living Guru (Mahmood 2013: 67–77).

Not only are the sacred texts themselves different across the faiths, within a given corpus, people could draw on different portions of these texts to support particular positions with regard to killing. Some people argue that religious texts have nothing to say about politics. The problem, however, is often the opposite. They have too many teachings about politics, and the modern believer has to choose which texts apply in particular circumstances (Birdsall and Rowley 2019).

Most religions have violence in their sacred texts. Texts revered by Hindus contain many battle scenes, most famously one where Arjuna seeks guidance from Krishna, who informs Arjuna that some forms of killing do not constitute violence (Das 2013: 27). Similarly, there are Buddhist scriptures 'that uphold the notion of *ahimsa* (nonviolence) and equanimity. Nonetheless, like every other global religion, Buddhist traditions have adherents that commit violence and justify their acts with scriptures. These Buddhist scriptures either condone the use of violence or are hermeneutically ambiguous' (Jerryson 2013: 43). Judaism, Christianity and Islam have many texts on killing – whether historical accounts of warfare, admonitions to spiritual warfare or an anticipated cataclysmic denouement. The same Hebrew Bible texts can be used to promote war or peace (Eisen 2011). With Christian texts, peaceful images within the New Testament can morph under the pressure of politics and be turned towards the promotion of war (Martin 2006). The Qur'an, when read chronologically, shows a slow transition from years of patient suffering to embracing the conditional use of the sword (Lawrence 2013: 126–31). These later 'sword verses' play an important part in modern Islamic terrorism. The trajectory in Bahá'í texts is different, with a few early texts offering a highly qualified endorsement of the use of force and the subsequent texts unambiguously condemning killing (Stockman 2020: 4).

Battles in sacred texts lend themselves to being inhabited. Habitation occurs when individuals or groups use a particular warfare text to deeply shape their understanding of a current conflict. Deeply inhabiting a text involves more than noting similarities between a text and a current circumstance; it involves a close identification with the text in a way that substantially shapes how a conflict is interpreted. When some people identify with righteous warriors in Scripture, their enemies blur with enemies described in that text. When this happens, it becomes easier to view flesh and blood enemies as symbols acting in a drama rather than as humans who have particular reasons for engaging in conflict or seeking peace (Rowley 2024). Sometimes a group might believe it is a divinely chosen or elected people living on sacred land, just like a group in Scripture (O'Brien 1988). One can also inhabit texts in ways that push individuals or groups away from violence. Sometimes the same text can have both effects. For example, the exodus and conquest narrative in the Hebrew Bible has been put to many uses across the centuries (Coffey 2014). Most who inhabit this narrative never use the text for violence, but the text has a long history of being used as a mental framework in warfare. People like Martin Luther King Jr. have also used the account to frame the non-violent struggle for dignity and rights.

Within the same sacred corpus, many exemplars 'modelled' different relationships with violence (Eller 2010: 74–5). This diversity foregrounds an important question: why do post-scriptural believers, in certain circumstances, identify with a violent exemplar over one who promoted peace? Most believers are not pushed towards violence by their text, and other non-religious factors often push a small subset of believers to think a violent application is an authentic expression of faith (Jenkins 2012: 252).

There is no straight or necessary connection between texts and violence. We must navigate between viewing sacred texts as passive (acted upon by later humans) and humans as passive (acted upon by texts). Readers and texts influence each other (Nelson 2010: 5). We can also learn a lot about a person (or the situation they are in) by their choice of a violent text over a loving, merciful or forgiving one. The same text might lead adherents from the same tradition into radically different actions. For example, submission and rebellion could both be supported by an appeal to Romans 13:1–4. The submissive note what authority *is* (ordained by God). Rebels note what legitimate authority *is for* (ordained by God for the purpose of approving of right actions and punishing wrong ones). When authority is unjust, it loses its divine ordination.

3.6 Supernatural and Human Agency

From antiquity to the present, People from differing creeds claimed that more-than-human forces or agents have participated in their conflicts (Rowley and Hodgson 2022). There are many conceptions about how nature and supernature relate and how or why more-than-human agents or forces might participate in conflict (through natural processes, contrary to natural processes, etc.).

There are also divergent beliefs about how humans may influence, or be influenced by, these forces or agents. Many faith traditions believe that God communicates through events, and victory or defeat are often interpreted as divinely wrought. Some believe that beneficent more-than-human agency in war is predicated on the correct beliefs of participants ('God fights for the orthodox'). Others might emphasise how supernatural participation depends on the particular circumstances of a conflict ('God fights on the side of justice'). Those who believe they have orthodox beliefs and a just cause might hope for a double blessing.

One should watch carefully when an individual or group claims divine participation in their controversial activity. They may downplay human action ('We did nothing') or emphasise divine activity ('This is the Lord's doing'). Such statements shift the responsibility from the human to the divine.

How do these forces or agents influence conflict? Sometimes sacred objects are instrumental (talismans, icons or relics) and sometimes this agency is tied to particular locations (sacred spaces) or to particular times of the year (sacred dates) or to people (prophets, saints). Sometimes divine agency in war is thought to work independently of human agents, sometimes through human instruments and at other times alongside them. Sometimes divine assistance merely takes the form of divine assent (as when a religious leader proclaims God's approval). At other times the claim is much more specific (as when a religious leader claims God sent a specific natural disaster to thwart the enemy). Finally, some believe the divine is beyond human manipulation, while others argue divine forces are manipulatable through ritual or feats of devotion. In traditional African religions, the gods are often considered pliable, and thus humans are responsible for their use of divine power (Wlodarczyk 2013: 153–66).

3.7 Religion–State Relations

Religious institutions often act as alternative sources of authority and can present a buffer between individuals and the state. Intermediary institutions can influence the masses towards submission or resistance; towards war or peace. In the same way, states can use intermediaries to influence individuals. Unsurprisingly, many secular regimes remove religious intermediaries, giving the state a monopoly on authority.

Many regions of the world have been characterised by political fragmentation, and religious and cultural diversity sometimes contributes to conflict. However, a centralised and powerful state solves some problems but creates others. The overwhelming size and power of the Chinese state across millennia has led to comparatively few wars over 'religion' (but not the absence of 'religion' from wars). The Christianity-influenced Taiping Rebellion is a notable exception. 'Neither Buddhism, nor Daoism, nor the popular religion, have been able to establish [religious structures] of lasting political, economic, or military influence. The institutional impotence of the Chinese faiths has been due to the enormous clout of the imperial – or, recently, communist – regimes' (Shahar 2013: 188). When the state dominates in this way, religious groups are often limited in their ability to critique government abuse or check state ambitions.

There are many ways that a particular faith tradition, in a specific time and place, might relate to a particular civil order (e.g. evangelical Christians in Palestine might hold different beliefs about the state use of force than evangelical Christians in the United States). A particular civil order may have different ways of relating to the various religious groups (e.g. the Iranian government favours the Shia and persecutes the Bahá'í). Each variation has important implications for when and why lethal force might be deemed permissible.

(1) Sometimes, a religious community has significant control over the levers of power, and religious leaders might hold positions of authority in both spheres. The controversial term 'theocracy' is often applied to such arrangements. In these cases, it isn't easy to differentiate between the policies of the state and those of the faith. The state may punish religious infractions. The religious community is viewed as largely co-terminous with the political community, and the state becomes sacred through its close association with religion.

(2) In other societies, a religious community is in the process of securing control over civil power in the manner described in the previous paragraph. Such societies experience high levels of conflict, with not only a civil order that might prefer independence but also the wider society that may not desire the conflating of civil and religious spheres.

(3) There are often high levels of cooperation between civil and religious authorities. This cooperation may constitute a mild or informal establishment of a particular religion. In this case, the civil society and the religious community may not be co-terminous, but 'true' or 'full' members of the society belong to the favoured faith. In the first three examples, religion risks becoming an organ of the state, and the religious are often unable or unwilling to critique the state and its use of violence meaningfully.

(4) Sometimes, the power dynamics are reversed, and the civil power dominates, or seeks to dominate, the religious order. The civil power not only functions as the arbiter of disputes between competing religions, it also determines dogma. The civil and religious communities are often co-terminous, and religious disagreement is tantamount to a crime against the state. Similarly, some secular polities have historically sought to dominate or expel religious adherents.

(5) Related to the previous position, many civil orders view religious dissenters as a threat – whether they are in society or separated from it. Political leaders may allow them to remain, but only under severe restrictions. Other leaders may argue that dissenters are dangerous to the wider society and must be removed.

(6) Some religious groups retreat from civil society because they believe faith requires separation or as a practical means to maintain doctrinal or communal purity. The wider society may view this separation as a threat.

(7) Finally, some civil orders aim to be neutral referees that grant considerable latitude to a plurality of faith communities. The state limits direct involvement in religion, and religious communities are to limit their expectations for how the state should reflect their values. Religious communities are allowed to compete for adherents, provided conversions are not forced, adherents are not subject to violence and can leave the group and as long as outsiders are not physically attacked. When the state steps in, it is often to arbitrate disputes between religious communities or to proscribe a limited set of religious practices (like polygamy), even when these practices may be rooted in a faith tradition.

The differences between these positions are partly due to divergent political structures, the theology of various religious groups and the unique history of religion–state relations in a given region. Further, debates about conscience and religious toleration are intricately tied up with the above positions, with groups on one end of the spectrum arguing that true faith can never be coerced and others arguing that it is charitable to push people into the fold or to purge dissenters from the body-politic by execution or expulsion.

Religion and the state are related in another key respect. Most religions exist in more than one nation, and many are liberally spread across the globe. Religious communities are dispersed for many reasons (missionary work, colonisation, slavery, displacement due to war or famine, education or financial opportunities). Some religions may actively try to convert peoples in distant lands, an act that is often interpreted as hostile by political or religious authorities. Global religions foster supranational networks. When there is persecution in one region, co-religionists worldwide may deeply identify with those who suffer and develop animosities towards those who inflict the suffering. Religions strengthen ties of sympathy around the globe, even as they redraw global boundaries between in-group and out-group.

3.8 Personal Eschatology

What happens to killers and those killed after death? Most religious traditions believe that there is a next state of existence and that the condition of future existence is predicated in some way on beliefs or behaviours in this life. The condition of the next state could involve a higher or lower reincarnation, movement towards or away from enlightenment or residence in a final (or sometimes temporary) destination of paradise or perdition. The promise of reward and the fear of punishment is deeply, but ambivalently, related to beliefs about killing. People may have self-interested reasons to eschew violence and work towards peace. Someone may even accept martyrdom as a pathway to rewards, and martyrdom involves accepting an unjust death. Personal eschatology may also provide self-interested reasons to intensify conflict and justify killing. Someone may link martyrdom and rewards, and martyrdom involves the taking of lives or dying on the battlefield. There is much confusion in the scholarly literature about how other-worldly rewards relate to the justification of lethal force, and we must distinguish between two broad ways of relating the two. In one variant, the faithful are told they will be rewarded *although* they engage in war or die in battle. In a more alarming variant, the faithful are told they will be rewarded *because* they engage in war or die in battle. In the second, the killing itself is meritorious.

Whereas states can use terror against other states or even their own citizens, the use of terror by non-state actors is a relatively recent development. Many religious and non-religious traditions have justified suicide terrorism. Heavenly rewards are not the motivation for the non-religious, even as they may appeal to a transcendent cause. Scholars trace modern terrorism to anarchist movements in Revolutionary France, and the tactic was also widely used in Germany, Russia and Ireland. Terrorism of this sort has a long association with followers of Marx and Lenin, and eventually, *suicide* terrorism would become a recognised and seemingly effective way to force political change (Forst 2009: 44–59). Suicide terrorism, it has been argued, dates back to the biblical Sampson, but it was not widely practised until World War II. A particularly influential embrace of suicide involved Japanese kamikaze bombers who fought on behalf of the state religion, Shinto (Skya 2011: 227–36). In 1972, the anti-Israel Japanese Red Army (a Marxist/Leninist anti-imperial group also known as the Holy War Brigade) were responsible for what has been called the 'first contemporary suicide attack in the Middle East' (Jerryson 2013: 41–2). Thus, although the Abrahamic faiths have been involved in terror and suicide terrorism, modern terrorism has deep roots in secularism and non-Abrahamic faith.

3.9 Visions of the End

Just as views about the creation of the natural order influence beliefs about killing, visions of the end likewise impact conflict in the present. Some traditions, like Buddhism, emphasise the cyclical nature of time, but it is a cycle leading towards an age of destruction. This belief has given rise to violent Buddhist millenarian movements (Jerryson 2013: 56–7). Similarly, Hindu eschatology emphasises cycles of dissolution and rebirth, and a future avatar of Vishnu will bring about cataclysmic purging (LaRocca 1996: 3–12). Other traditions emphasise the destination towards which history is heading, a culminating moment that is redemptive or destructive (and sometimes both). Many in the Abrahamic traditions believe that human agents should work in some way to bring about this end, and this 'work' can take the form of promoting right practices, proselytising, doing charitable deeds or furthering justice and peace on earth. A subset within these traditions may believe they need to force the end by hastening conflict or embracing killing to move history towards its appointed goal. Most of the scriptural literature in the Abrahamic tradition is backwards-looking – telling the deeds and teachings of people like Moses, Jesus or Muhammad. Eschatological literature tends to be interpreted as forward-looking. Thus, it is easy for people to 'inhabit' such texts – to live within the text because they believe the text describes the moment they live in. When conflict arises, the event can be fitted into a long-anticipated schema and it becomes easier to view enemies as symbols in an apocalyptic drama and as an obstacle to a glorious future.

4 Can Holy War Ever Be Just?

Section 2 surveyed competing ways of understanding killing in God's name. Scholars try to identify harmful aspects of faith and quarantine beliefs and practices that seem especially prone to extremism and violence. What if much of this scholarship is asking the wrong question? This section shifts the question from 'is this a dangerous belief' or 'is this religious violence?' to a more productive one: 'what is the relationship between justice and holiness in this lethal act?' This section opens with the 'Muslim Police Officer Dilemma', noting how an officer could describe the same lethal act using language drawn from the 'religious' or 'secular' registers. In the officer's mind, the sacred and secular provide two compatible ways of viewing the same lethal act. However, he might avoid articulating religious language because he fears misinterpretation.

I then modify a classic dilemma, calling it 'Euthyphro's Military Dilemma': 'Is a lethal act considered holy because it is just or just because it is holy?' Our traditional 'one-dimensional' approach to killing in the name of religion does not help us unravel this dilemma, so I propose a 'three-dimensional' approach. There are two primary ways Euthyphro could relate justice to holiness. Sometimes partisans claimed Scripture or belief in God's will *constructed* the reasons to participate in a particular conflict (what I call constructivism). Constructivists believe violence is just because it is holy (holy, therefore just war). At other times people argued that participation in a particular conflict was *compatible* with or *corresponded* to Scripture or God's will (what I call compatibilism). Compatibilists believe violence is holy because it is just (just, therefore holy war). Scholars commit a grave error when they mistake the two. I will argue that constructivism is the more alarming variant and offer some guidance on detecting it.

4.1 The Muslim Police Officer Dilemma

Religious people can use language and ideas from two registers – what might be imperfectly called 'secular' and 'sacred' – to justify or describe their use of force. How are the discourses related? Many observers of violence in God's name treat religious justifications for violence as if they exerted something akin to *genetic dominance* over an act of killing. Consider the biology of baby-making. If a mother has brown eyes and the father has blue, the brown eyes are dominant and will usually present in the child. People will say the baby 'has her mother's eyes'. The recessive allele remains uncommented upon. In the same way, many observers of violence treat the religious components (brown) as dominant, often ignoring what might be termed secular components (blue). This foregrounding of the religious components often confirms the biases of the observer and the particular theology they oppose.

This approach might be called the 'one drop rule of religious violence'. Just as racist legal practice in the United States made 'one drop' of African blood decisive in legally defining an individual's race, some make one drop of religion in a lethal act decisive in identifying the motivation of the killer. An act is 'religious violence' if they detect a trace of religion. For example, many people wrongly assume that 'all violence involving Muslims – regardless of whether they are the aggressor or the victim – is "Muslim Violence"' (Atwill 2007: 126).

When the 'one drop' rule is applied, atheist school shooters are accused of 'implicit' religious violence (Pfeifer and Ganzevoort 2014: 447–59) and the agnostic terrorist Timothy McVeigh is the poster boy for homegrown Christian radicalism (rightly critiqued in Armstrong 2014: 312; Stark and Corcoran 2014: 26–7, 40; Mason 2015: 219). The mass suicide promoted by Jim Jones (Jonestown) is frequently deemed 'religious', but the classification is complicated because he was a Methodist minister who was also a professing atheist and Marxist (Armstrong 2014: 308). In the case of Jones, was there a dominant 'religious' or 'atheist' allele, and how would one decide? Unlike in biology, human beliefs and motivations make it harder to differentiate dominant from recessive.

Before delving into large-scale conflicts, imagine a small-scale lethal act (the 'Muslim Police Officer Dilemma'). Let us imagine that a Christian Nationalist in New Zealand is holding Muslims captive in a mosque. The recent Christchurch mosque massacre reminds everyone that the death toll could be catastrophic. The terrorist threatens to shoot hostages, and authorities decide to act, sending in one sniper. They happen to choose a Muslim. This Muslim is tasked with killing a person who claims to be lethally defending Christianity. The officer is not only defending civilians; he is defending co-religionists, defending their right to worship without fear, defending religion itself. Should the officer's act be classified as religious violence? Is this a *good* form of religious violence?

The officer uses lethal force, and afterwards this hero sits down for an interview with a major national broadcaster. He describes his actions in a secular way:

> 'When the command from my superior came, I had a duty to act'
> 'I could not let him kill these innocent people'
> 'The assailant needed to be brought to justice'

New Zealand's Muslim community was also proud of their hero, and he sat down with a religious news outlet. He gave a very different interview, mainly drawing from the sacred register:

'Just as Allah was with the Prophet, peace be upon him, I knew Allah was with me'
'Allah wanted me to prevent this evil and stop this attack upon Islam'
'Religion was at stake'
'After I saw the terrorist was dead, I whispered "Allahu akbar"'
'My imam told me I was Allah's instrument'
'I knew my actions were holy and pleased Allah'

I call this a 'dilemma' because the officer might feel pressure from secular society to downplay his religious understanding of the event. In the public sphere, could this Muslim officer express his deep conviction in Allah's providence without leaving himself open to misinterpretation? An uncharitable interpreter might accuse him of blending religion and violence or of viewing his actions through the frame of cosmic war.

In this scenario, the Muslim officer comes close to Roland Bainton's classic definition of a holy warrior ('holy warrior' in the pejorative sense) – a definition that is as influential as it is misguided:

[A] The crusading idea requires that the cause shall be holy (and no cause is more holy than religion) [B] that the cause shall be fought under God and with his help, [C] that the crusaders shall be godly and their enemies ungodly, [D] and that the war shall be prosecuted unsparingly. (Bainton 1960: 148, brackets added)

The officer believed that killing this Christian was holy, he believed that Allah was with him, he believed that the terrorist was an enemy of Allah and the officer unsparingly took the assailant's life.

In his two interviews, this Muslim officer gave very different explanations for his actions. To treat the religious component as dominant would be to misunderstand how sacred and secular relate in the mind of the officer. As will be argued later, this officer believed his actions were both just and holy – indeed just, *therefore* holy. His sacred rationale *complemented* and *corresponded* to his secular rationale.

Similar scenarios play out in real life. Consider a 2017 shooting in a Texas church, the deadliest attack on worshipers in United States history. The terrorist was described as a zealous and aggressive evangelist for atheism (BBC News 2017). After hearing gunfire, Stephen Willeford grabbed his firearm and wounded the terrorist, who fled the scene. Willeford chased him, and the assailant died of his wounds (some of them self-inflicted). The hero believed that his actions as a citizen – taking his rifle, shooting a stranger and preventing his escape – were just.

Willeford also viewed his actions through a religious frame: the terrorist was demonic (Holley 2020: 136). Willeford praised God for protection and for giving him lethal skills (Roberts and Cole 2017). Living in the southern United States, he probably felt little pressure to conceal his religious understanding of the event, and he was widely hailed as a 'good Samaritan'. Were Willeford's lethal actions just or holy? Doubtless, he would have answered 'Both'. The religious frame did not detract from the secular one – it intensified it.

The fictitious Muslim police officer and the Texas church shooting are morally simple narratives. None but the strictest pacifists would object to the police officer's lethal act. And even though Willeford acted without commands from authority, most would consider his actions just. The examples offer an analytical clarity and simplicity that rarely appears in geopolitics. They demonstrate a simple point: in many lethal acts that invoke God or religion, ideas about justice closely correspond to ideas about holiness. In both examples, the ones who brought an end to unjust killing believed their actions were just and therefore holy. They did not argue that their actions were holy and therefore just. It is necessary to make such distinctions if we desire to understand violence that invokes God and religion.

4.2 Euthyphro Marches to War

One question in the literature from classical antiquity continues to intrigue many who encounter it. Plato recorded a dialogue between Socrates and Euthyphro, a dialogue about criminality and prosecution. Crime and punishment are closely related to sanctity and holiness, and the conversation drifted towards religion. Socrates asked Euthyphro what holiness is. Euthyphro said, 'the holy is doing what I'm now doing, prosecuting a wrongdoer'. Failure to prosecute is 'unholy' (Plato 2017, *Euthyphro*, LCL 36: 35, 37). Socrates charged Euthyphro with evading the question by describing a holy act (prosecuting a murderer) instead of defining what holiness is.

A deeper issue undergirded notions of holiness, knowledge (epistemology). How does one know an act is holy and thus not a crime? Euthyphro's answer linked knowledge of holiness with divinity: 'something that the gods love is holy and what they do not love is unholy'. Given Grecian polytheism and the mercurial gods, this solution was unsuitable. Socrates noted how competing gods 'consider different things to be just, and honorable and shameful, and good and bad' (Plato 2017, *Euthyphro*, LCL 36: 41, 45). He then sharpened the question: 'is the holy loved by the gods because it is holy, or is it holy because it is loved?' (Plato 2017, *Euthyphro*, LCL 36: 55). In other words, does the love of the gods *correspond* to holiness, or does their love *construct* holiness?

What happens when Euthyphro steps out of the courtroom and marches to war? Socrates' question can be modified: Is a lethal act *just* because it is *holy*, or is it *holy* because it is *just*? The remainder of this section explores the difference between these positions and argues that discerning this difference is crucial for understanding lethal acts that have a religious component.

4.3 Pacifism, Just War and Holy War

Humans are classifying animals and often resort to prefabricated categories when they see lethal force. Anti-war protestors are slotted into the 'Pacifism' file. Ukrainian forces' killing of Russian soldiers goes in the 'Just War' file. And killings by the group commonly called 'Islamic State' go in the 'Holy War' file. Such categorisation is a normal form of shorthand, and the one doing the sorting uses both intuition and evidence when deciding where to place each act. These three categories are sometimes placed on a spectrum.

This spectrum allows for a degree of nuance. One can imagine, for example, something between 'Pacifism' and 'Just War' – maybe a highly restrained defensive war. Again, one can imagine something between 'Just War' and 'Holy War' – maybe a complicated war where issues of justice are at stake, but religious leaders try to pervert the cause (Allman 2008: 18).

However, there are significant problems with this spectrum, problems that fundamentally obscure the relationship between religion and the use of lethal force. First, a spectrum is zero-sum: as a conflict moves closer to 'Holy War', it necessarily moves away from 'Just War' and even further from 'Pacifism'. Thus, as per the zero-sum approach, the conflict contains less 'justice' for every bit of 'holiness' injected into it. Justice and holiness appear to be in opposition, and indeed many scholars write as if the opposite of a just warrior is a holy warrior. However, the opposite of a just warrior is an unjust warrior. Second, 'Pacifism' is a rejection of violence. On this spectrum, 'Holy War' appears to be the opposite of restrained – a superabundance of violence. However, 'holy warriors' often have deeply religious reasons to limit violence and 'just warriors' have shed a prodigious amount of blood. 'Just War' is not necessarily less lethal than 'Holy War', as its relative position closer to 'Pacifism' seems to indicate. Both assumptions are evident in

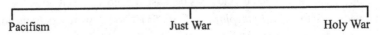

Pacifism   Just War   Holy War

Figure 2 One-dimensional view of conflict

President Obama's 2009 Nobel Peace Prize address where he claimed 'that no Holy War can ever be a just war', strongly linking holy warfare with indiscriminate and excessive bloodshed (New York Times 2009). Rather than the one-dimensional spectrum, I propose a three-dimensional approach.

4.4 A Three-Dimensional View of Warfare

'Pacifism', 'Just War' and 'Holy War' do not belong on a single spectrum. Instead, each deserves its own: 'Pacifism' belongs on a spectrum relating to the 'Use of Lethal Force'; 'Just War' on one relating to 'Claimed Justice'; and 'Holy War' on one relating to 'Claimed Holiness'. These spectrums are often intertwined – many argue that justice is indispensable to holiness or that there is a religious grounding to justice – but they can be separated for analytical purposes.

Level of Lethal Force: The vertical spectrum relates to the amount of lethal force deemed permissible or actually employed and who may be deemed an object of such force. A pacifist would be represented at the bottom of the vertical spectrum. Strict pacifists are unwilling to use lethal force, full stop. On the other end are those who believe that high levels of lethal force are permissible or required. They may even be reserved when resorting to war, but once the war is begun, restraint may be deemed counterproductive. They may even believe that targeting civilians is permissible or necessary.

In discussing this first spectrum, nothing has been said about 'justice' or 'holiness'. Some wars that are widely deemed just – like the Allied campaign in

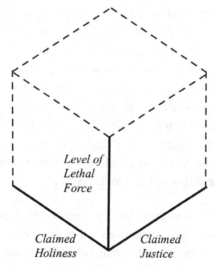

Figure 3 Three-dimensional view of conflict

WWII – featured high levels of violence and the targeting of civilians (most notably the firebombing of Dresden and the atomic destruction of Hiroshima and Nagasaki). Conversely, some conflicts that are deemed holy evidence great restraint precisely because God is involved and will hold combatants accountable. Beliefs about holiness or justice are not, of necessity, tied to a particular level of violence.

Claimed Justice: The right horizontal spectrum relates to how and why partisans claim their cause and actions are just. The word 'claimed' is important, for we are not evaluating whether actions were actually just, only why and how partisans thought they were. This spectrum relates to appeals to some form of public justice. On the right side of the spectrum are 'Robust Appeals to Justice'. Partisans on this end may justify their lethal force by appealing to commonly understood standards of justice (e.g. the inviolable nature of boundaries, the right of self-defence or the need to hold perpetrators to account). On the other end of the spectrum are 'Anaemic Appeals to Justice'. Those resorting to lethal force make little attempt to justify their actions by appeals to commonly understood standards of justice. Those who make robust appeals to justice and those whose appeals are anaemic can justify varying levels of lethal force.

It is important to listen for claims about justice, especially when someone claims their violence is holy. If we search for why someone thought their lethal force was *holy*, we are in danger of missing why they thought it was *just*. However, if we search for why they thought lethal action was *just*, we will likely gain deeper insights into why they thought it was *holy*. Consider Osama bin Laden, the quintessential advocate of religious warfare. He repeatedly framed his anger in terms of the violation of international standards of justice and blamed lukewarm Muslim nations and their godless (and simultaneously Christian) Western allies. Bin Laden had a long history of making justice-related complaints against the West (Khalil 2018: 36–48). However much one might want to nuance or rebut his charges, many of the claims are intelligible to someone who does not share his religious worldview. However, because Bin Laden couched his appeals to justice in the language of Islam, his anger could be ignored or dismissed as fanatical and irrational. However, he thought his cause was just, and those who care about global stability would be remiss if they failed to understand why and how he came to this conclusion.

Claimed Holiness: Our third spectrum is perhaps the most misunderstood. The various world religions have similarities and differences in understanding the holy, the divine, the sacred or the transcendent. Further, one need not be confessionally religious to hold beliefs that have significant overlap with concepts of holiness, the sacred or the transcendent. Communist regimes, for example, may discard or demonise religious belief and practice, but sacralisation easily migrates to politics (Slezkine 2017) and state-*sanctioned* lethality. Even words like 'sanctioned' are etymologically related to 'sacred' and *sanctus*. Sanctioning force and declaring force sacred are overlapping concepts.

Lethal acts are often justified with language that invokes the sacred because the perpetrator and the object are both human. Consider the 2022 Russian invasion of Ukraine. President Vladimir Putin invoked Christianity to justify and describe his actions. The Russian Orthodox Church supplied his regime with theological weapons. Conversely, Ukrainian ministers, who share many beliefs with their Russian counterparts, invoked the faith as they hardened their resolve against invasion. On both sides of this conflict, many ministers and combatants framed what they were doing in terms of the sacred and transcendent. A religious framing on both sides of this conflict suggests another important point of this third spectrum: the claim that one's cause is holy does not have a *necessary* relationship to publicly agreed-upon standards of justice. Although Russia claims its cause is both just and holy, 141 United Nations member states denounced their actions as unjust. Additionally, worldwide Christian leaders have challenged Russia's claim to holiness.

The one-dimensional spectrum flattened conflict by treating justice and holiness in a zero-sum manner and strongly correlating claims of holiness with unrestrained violence. The three-dimensional approach allows for greater nuance. Consider the following three illustrations.

Figure 4 shows little restraint (high level of violence). Perhaps partisans target civilians. Perhaps they use weapons that are largely banned by international agreements. Perhaps they manufacture conditions of scarcity that devastate populations. In this illustration, the partisans also evidence anaemic appeals to justice. They may say their cause is just, but most onlookers would dispute such claims. Perhaps they argue that an invasion is in the national interest. Perhaps they claim it will bring material benefits. Perhaps they claim the invaded territory should be theirs by right, citing some historical injustice. Outside responses to such claims evidence a chasm between their standard of justice and commonly received ones (even if such grounds for war might have been persuasive in previous centuries). The majority of the claims are not widely accepted by outsiders. Concurrently, partisans relate their cause to something transcendent – be that the will of God or the sacred destiny of the nation. Perhaps a religious authority has blessed the military enterprise. Perhaps scriptural verses seem to sanction the killing. Perhaps killing is deemed

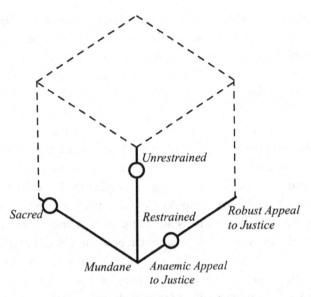

Figure 4 Unrestrained transcendent war

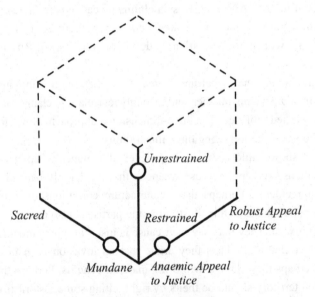

Figure 5 Meaningless war

necessary to bring about some anticipated renewal of the cosmos or to usher in a classless society.

Another type of conflict is marked by the lack of justifications for lethal force and little attempt to restrain lethal force (Figure 5). It is not called 'meaningless' because the violence has no meaning or justificatory logic but because the partisans attribute less meaning to their actions and aims in war. They make little attempt to justify their actions to the wider world and scarcely appeal to a larger transcendent cause. Perhaps they are motivated by personal ambition, a sense of personal injury or by a lust for bloodshed.

In this illustration, partisans offer robust appeals to justice. Perhaps they invoke territorial sovereignty or the right of self-determination. Perhaps partisans speak of self-defence or the need to protect the defenceless. Perhaps they appeal to international charters that stipulate the proper relations between nations. In sum, they appeal to widely received standards of justice. As this illustration shows, they also make robust appeals to the holy, sacred or the transcendent. In addition to caring about international charters, perhaps they also care about what is revealed in sacred writ. Religious authority may say all theft is denounced in Scripture, and this proscription also applies to thefts perpetrated by nations. Clergy may claim that God deems it praiseworthy to defend the innocent, even if that involves taking someone's life. Partisans in this type of conflict view their cause and actions as both just and holy. Convictions about justice and holiness often regulate behaviour in war, including the use of force. Because partisans strive for justice and holiness, there are some things that one simply does not do to another human (even if that human is an enemy). However, religious beliefs can also loosen restraints. Perhaps an individual believes God will forgive or reward indiscriminate killing. Perhaps highly valuing the lives of the righteous means

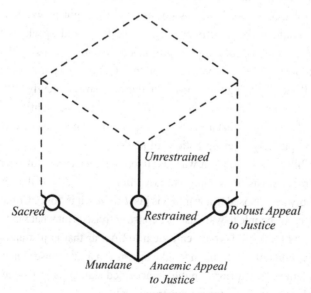

Figure 6 Just and holy warfare

that the lives of the unrighteous are insignificant. Thus, a warrior who makes robust appeals to holiness may be restrained or unrestrained.

In sum, this section argued that the single-spectrum understanding of religion and violence is inadequate. We need a three-dimensional approach that utilises separate but related spectrums: levels of lethal force might be high or low; partisans might make anaemic or robust appeals to public justice; and they might closely relate their cause to the holy, sacred or transcendent or think of their cause in a mundane this-worldly way.

4.5 Two Solutions to Euthyphro's Wartime Dilemma

Earlier, we left our Greek companion, Euthyphro, contemplating an important question as he marched to war: Is a lethal act *just* because it is *holy*, or is it *holy* because it is *just*? We are now better positioned to understand two ways Euthyphro might respond.

First, Euthyphro might say the holiness in the cause *created* or *constructed* the just cause. The sense of justice was largely derived from beliefs related to holiness and the sacred. Euthyphro (as a constructivist) might make simplistic appeals to a sacred text and argue that a certain text creates the right to kill. He might invest lethal authority in religious leaders, noting how an act is right because God's representative commands it. He might even go to God and claim that the right to take life derives directly from the leading of God through special revelation. These appeals, which could be multiplied, relate to sacred texts, sacred authority and the direct sense of the divine.

Instead of arguing that holiness constructed the right to use lethal force, Euthyphro could make a different argument. He could speak in terms of *compatibility*. As described above, *constructivists* may invoke sacred texts, sacred authority and the direct sense of the divine. *Compatibilists* can also appeal to these same legitimations, but they do so differently. Rather than argue that an interpretation of the sacred text creates the right to go to war, the *compatibilist* argues that arguments from Scripture need to correspond to or complement publicly received notions of justice.

Compatibilists link God and war just like constructivists. But what kind of war do compatibilists think God would participate in? A war that is just and *therefore* holy (as opposed to a war that is just *because* it is holy). Compatibilists think God 'calls' people to war, just like constructivists. But what kind of war do compatibilists think God would call them to? A war that is just and *therefore* holy. God would only 'call' them to take up arms in a just cause. Thus, a divine call could tether the warrior to publicly accepted standards of justice (compatibilist) or loose him from them (constructivist).

Constructivists tend to turn the religious 'other' into an enemy; compatibilists argue that grave, unremedied injustices made one an enemy and confirmed outsider status. For example, one sixteenth-century English Protestant could justify war with Catholics in Spain because Catholics were associated with the antichrist (constructivist). Another English Protestant might argue that Spanish Catholics proved they were doctrinally allied with the antichrist when they tried to physically conquer the British Isles and restore Catholicism (compatibilist). Both might arrive at the same conclusion that God supported war with Spain, but the compatibilist makes more robust arguments related to justice.

Both constructivists and compatibilists might praise God for how war afforded the opportunity to spread the faith. A constructivist might argue that war was justified *so that* another nation might be punished for beliefs and then evangelised. A compatibilist might argue that a just war *presented the occasion* when a foreign nation might be punished for beliefs and then evangelised. Both might see the war as a part of a God-ordained conversion plan, though their meaning was quite different.

The two positions are also evident in how laws are made and who has the right to rule. A constructivist might argue that the godliest party should have political authority. Doubtless, they believe godly leaders would further justice and foster stability. When they make laws, constructivist reason from divine law to state law (because something is in sacred writ, it should also be the law of the land). A compatibilist might also think that God elevated them to power, but they recognise how human institutions (hereditary succession, democratic election, etc.) could have placed someone less godly in leadership, and these leaders would have been equally legitimate. They do not try to erase the tension between divine law and state law. While they may want sacred convictions to be reflected in human law, they recognise limitations on fulfilling this desire and respect other sources of legal authority. Ideally, a single law could be grounded through two discourses: from secular law and from sacred convictions. Indeed, they argue that such laws have greater force because two different rationales legitimate them.

Although there are overlaps between the two approaches, correspondence seems to be the more common variant. Constructivism is the more alarming one, precisely because the right to rule, legislate and kill is primarily derived from sacred rationales. I suspect that most people who claim a divine calling to join the military or praise God for raising up a political leader or cite Scripture to justify a law are thinking in terms of correspondence ('I am willing to fight for just causes'; 'all authority is of God and I am glad this leader is godly'; 'this law furthers justice as Scripture confirms'). After we recognise that such statements are relatively normal, then we can begin to discern when and why other believers are constructing the right to kill almost exclusively on sacred beliefs and texts. If we do not make such distinctions, we will have a hard time differentiating the alarming signal (constructivism) from the noise (compatibilism).

This section is deeply indebted to my scholarship on the history of Christian warfare (Rowley 2024). I suspect there are similarities in other religious traditions. Perhaps, too, similar distinctions exist among the secular. Some secularists might ground their right to govern, coerce and kill on the notion that they possess enlightened 'orthodox' ideals (constructivism). Other secularists might argue that their enlightened bona fides equip them to enforce and protect ideals that secularists and many religious people alike widely share, and a religious person could also hold such authority (compatibilism).

5 Does Extremism Enable or Restrain Violence?

What makes a belief or action extreme? Who decides what is extreme, and how did they acquire such authority? Is the danger in holding beliefs firmly, dogmatically and uncompromisingly ('I am undoubtedly right'), or does the extremism lie in the content of belief ('Unbelievers have no right to live')? Can moderation also be a handmaiden to violence? Is there such a thing as nonviolent extremism, and might it be an antidote to violent extremism? To tackle these questions, we will start with the example of someone whose faith motivated their use of lethal force.

5.1 An Extreme Fight for Human Equality

In the late 1850s, before the American Civil War, John Brown launched a series of extrajudicial killings that targeted slaveholders. He then assaulted a federal arsenal. He was captured, tried and executed. Brown aimed to strike fear into slaveholders and spark a slave insurrection. He was a deeply religious man in the mould of the Puritan Oliver Cromwell. He argued for racial and gender equality and an immediate end to slavery with a single-minded biblically saturated passion. At the time, his religiously grounded vision of human equality was unmatched (see sources in Trodd and Stauffer 2004). In the wider Atlantic world of the time, 'moderate' and 'respectable' Christianity tolerated slavery while 'fanatic' and 'evangelical' abolitionism sought greater equality.

Some argued that slavery would have died out in a generation or two without Brown. Brown believed another half-century of slavery meant another half-century of whipped backs, raped women and separated families. For Brown, there was no morally neutral option. If he failed to act lethally for the benefit of enslaved humans, slaveholders would continue to act violently against them. The Golden Rule demanded action (Carlson and Ebel 2012: 1). If slaves had a natural right to fight for freedom – even though such action was against the law – did Brown have a right to fight on their behalf?

There is much to critique about Brown's planning, tactics and expectations. Much of the criticism is directed at his use of violence to kill pro-slavery civilians. Few were indifferent to Brown's ideas and actions. He was condemned in the South but garnered more sympathy in the North and even praise from Europe, where Victor Hugo compared his execution with that of Christ. However, many of Brown's abolitionist sympathisers critiqued his resort to violence. It was difficult to unreservedly praise someone who stepped outside authority structures and killed civilians (see sources in Trodd and Stauffer 2004: 173–268).

'Controversy over how to remember – or even depict or describe – John Brown and his legacy vexed American culture at the time of his death and continues to do so today', writes John D. Carlson and Jonathan H. Ebel (2012: 9). Some modern white Americans are embarrassed by Brown's fanaticism and violence, especially because his legacy has been appropriated for modern lethal causes. However, if Brown was a terrorist, his biographer David S. Reynolds notes, he was an '*American* terrorist in the amplest sense of the word, because he believed in the American ideal of equal rights for all, regardless of creed or race' (2005: 503).

Despite the ambiguous response from white Americans, Brown remains one of the most revered whites among modern African Americans. For example, he has been highly praised by giants of the African American intellectual tradition like W. E. B. Du Bois, Lerone Bennett Jr. and Cornel West. More than any other white person, perhaps, Brown identified with African Americans and suffered with them (Olsen 2011: 488).

This section explores extreme beliefs and the rejection or limitation of violence while also interrogating modern notions of 'extreme' and 'moderate'. Brown might seem out of place here, but he exemplifies some ambiguity around notions of extreme and moderate beliefs. He was an extremist for racial equality at a time when moderation meant allowing the enslavement of humans en masse. His faith led him to radical conclusions about what the love of one's neighbour might entail, namely that defending African neighbours might require killing white ones. He complicates modern understandings of 'restrained' and 'violent'. Brown was charged with 'extreme' and 'unrestrained' killing. However, the American Civil War (a war that cost the lives of hundreds of thousands of soldiers and civilians) is considered necessary, rational and morally praiseworthy (for the North, at least). If Brown had waited a few years and enlisted in the Northern Army, he might have killed exponentially more people – soldiers and 'collateral' civilians – and come home and been unreservedly praised for it.

5.2 The Danger of Apathetic Faith

In response to religiously motivated violence, many have argued that 'moderate faith' or no-faith is the solution. After 9/11, the New Atheists vigorously opposed those who took their faith too seriously. Richard Dawkins quotes Voltaire, who said, 'Those who can make you believe absurdities can make you commit atrocities'. Fervent faith is dangerous. But Dawkins also argues that 'the teachings of "moderate" religion, though not extremist in themselves, are an open invitation to extremism' (2006: 306). Moderate faith is also dangerous. Dawkin's solution is conversion to rationalism. Yet the history of the twentieth century shows a disturbing track record for regimes based on rationality. It turns out that those who can make you believe religions are absurdities can also make you commit atrocities.

Many religious leaders are keenly aware of the dangers of both faith and reason; however, secular leaders are often only aware of the dangers of faith. Pope Benedict XVI (then Cardinal Ratzinger) argued this point with Jürgen Habermas. He said there are 'pathologies in religion' and 'pathologies of reason' that prove very dangerous when either religion or reason reigns unchallenged (2005: 77–9). Faith and reason, sacred and secular, are not only intertwined – the world needs them to work together.

Dawkins is right about the link between religious moderation and religious extremism, but the correlation is more complicated. He correctly notes how extremists often weaponise the beliefs that are widely held by moderates (Hamid 2016: 11), and thus moderate beliefs can be a seedbed for extremism. For example, most Christians believe the Bible contains teachings about the end of the world, but only a very small number think they should aggressively hasten this end through violent confrontation. Dawkins might throw out all eschatological thinking, root and branch.

However, moderate beliefs can also be dangerous precisely because the adherents are apathetic towards or indifferent to fervent religion. Consider white supremacist militia groups in the United States who adopt Christian names, use Christian symbols and claim to protect Christian heritage (Belew 2018). Christianity primarily serves as a cultural identity marker dividing 'us' from 'them', and these militants drain the faith of substantive theological content. The agnostic Timothy McVeigh is a case in point (Mason 2015: 219). When onlookers see Christian symbols used by white supremacist organisations, they assume that robust theology animates those wearing the symbols. However, leaders and members often possess a very thin understanding of Christian history and theology. A similar pattern appears in Europe, where the *irreligious* are particularly prone to joining right-wing groups that use Christian language and symbols. Many on the far-right even use Christian arguments (immigrants threaten Christian identity) against Christian teachings (Christianity teaches the love of the stranger). Indeed, the church has often criticised what is being promoted in its name (Cremer 2018).

The strongest arguments against weaponised faith come from within the faith. Devout Muslims are strongly positioned to critique Islamic terrorism (Akyol 2011). After 9/11, many leading Muslims condemned terrorist actions and theology, and these critics rooted their revulsion in sacred texts and Islamic history (Khalil 2018: 62–74). The New Atheists ignored such condemnations (Khalil 2018: 116–20) or dismissed them as 'inauthentic'. For example, Dawkins claimed the mantle as the discerner of authentic Muslim faith, even as he condescendingly asked of terrorism-denouncing Muslim clerics, 'who elected *them*, by the way?' (Dawkins 2006: 306–7).

Dawkins wants to push people from extreme/moderate religion into the rationalist camp. He does so by portraying terrorism as the authentic Muslim option. His arguments can be used to legitimise extremism. First, he demonises non-violent 'moderates' and needlessly drives a wedge between the flourishing of the secular state and the flourishing of religious practice. His thinking is zero-sum: tolerant Muslims become tolerant to the degree they move away from their faith. Second, Dawkins adopts and promotes the arguments of terrorists, namely that terrorism is the authentic expression of Islam (cf. Khalil 2018: 1). Given such statements from the New Atheists, is it any wonder that some Muslims consider the secular state to be hostile to their faith and find violence to be the authentic option for the besieged? Thankfully, *violent* extremism is only one of many expressions of fervent faith.

5.3 Returning to the Root of Faith

There are further reasons for interrogating contemporary notions of religious extremism: prodigious bloodshed has been justified in the name of 'moderation', and sometimes people have 'extreme' reasons for limiting or rejecting violence. First, the ideal of 'moderation' has a violent history. For example, Henry VIII provided a troubling image of moderation when, in 1540, he ordered the tying together of Catholic and Protestant ministers together before they were jointly hung in a 'grisly and calculated display of symmetry' (Shagan 2011: 73). In this case, the *via media* was the way of violence.

In the present, many calling for moderation want to push the religious towards conformity, enforce minimal public displays of religion or make bland theological identities the price of admission into a liberal democracy.

Advocates of moderation might try to weed out the 'wrong' sort of Muslims who take their faith too seriously (Fulford 2017) or only celebrate Jews who are not too Jewish (Horn 2021). Shadi Hamid notes the self-serving nature of calls for moderation when applied to Islam and politics: 'In popular discourse, [moderation] tends to translate roughly into doing the things we want Islamist groups to do'. Further, brutal autocratic regimes in the Middle East are called 'moderate', and Islamists who challenge the legitimacy of these regimes are deemed radical extremists (2014: 45–7; cf. 2016: 17; Akyol 2011). Indeed, 'the most politically influential Islamists groups have generally been of the mainstream and nonviolent variety', and the violent Islamists of the present 'are distinctively modern, perhaps *too* modern' (Hamid 2016: 6).

Religious groups can adopt a moderate stance for a variety of reasons. Sometimes moderation stems from religious convictions, sometimes it is imposed with a heavy hand, sometimes it is willingly adopted as a solution for living with pluralism and at other times, it might be a strategic move to avoid repression. Moderation has many meanings, and sometimes the 'moderate' have a monopoly on force and are unafraid to use it for illiberal ends.

Religious moderation is often linked with unremarkable beliefs. In this sense, moderates are like sheep shorn of objectionable convictions. They possess a theology devoid of miracles, divine retribution, moral and doctrinal absolutes, hierarchy and accountability, unerring sacred texts or eschatological anticipation. A moderate may privately believe such things but would not publicly speak about them. Moderate religion might seem more 'respectable', but it comes at the cost of removing much of a religion's resources for peace and human flourishing (Fulford 2017: 31). This 'domestication' of a religious tradition also makes it easier for those inclined to violence to paint the 'moderate' as inauthentic. Those inclined towards a robust theology are likely to spit out the moderate variation, as one might do with a traditional meal that is missing most of its ingredients. To dissuade those inclined towards violence, the alternative theology needs to taste right. The competing visions for religious faithfulness must be deeply *rooted* in the theological tradition (e.g. Akyol 2011).

The word 'radical' is etymologically related to 'roots' (*radix*). A radical might try to get to the root of a problem or find new solutions by returning to root principles. Scholars of violence debate the 'roots' of religion. Some argue that religion has corrupt 'roots' and is particularly prone to irrational violence. Others argue that religion has peaceful 'roots' that are conducive to human flourishing and that violence stems from a perversion of the faith by insincere actors. These rival interpretations of the 'root' are evident in debates about whether terrorism is un-Islamic or a true expression of Islam (Birdsall and Collins 2017: 1–4). Patrick Q. Mason argues that '[t]o argue that religion is either inherently violent or peaceful is to peddle in crass reductionism' (2015: 213). I concur.

Sometimes 'extreme' beliefs prevent violence; at other times 'extreme' beliefs foment conflict. Sometimes 'moderate' beliefs prevent violence; at other times 'moderate' beliefs allow injustice to reign unopposed. Judd Birdsall and Drew Collins make a similar point:

> seemingly radical instantiations of Islam and other world religions do not invariably lead to discrimination and violence. Religious conservatives can be political liberals. Theological exclusivists can be social inclusivists – precisely *because of*, not in spite of, their theological convictions. (Birdsall and Collins 2017: 2)

The history of religious pluralism counterintuitively shows how theologically closed-minded individuals greatly contributed to the development of universal toleration (Murphy 1997; cf. Rowley 2017).

Within each tradition, there is considerable disagreement over what lay at the 'root' of their faith. Traditions, in the present and across time, are internally pluralistic. Sacred texts, also, are diverse. For example, the portrait of a faithful Muslim has varied across time and space, and a given Muslim might emphasise or de-emphasise certain aspects of Islamic history and theology (Akyol 2011). There are multiple 'roots' or 'core' teachings within Judaism or Christianity that believers could draw on. Consider the Hebrew Bible. One could easily describe ritual purity or vengeance against outsiders as the essence of the faith. However, when Jesus was asked what lay at the heart of the Hebrew Bible, like many Jewish people before and after him, he pinpointed the love of God and neighbour (Deut. 6:5; Lev. 19:18; Matt. 22:36–40) – and the story of the Good Samaritan shows how expansive his definition of neighbour was (Luke 10:25–37). For the late Lord Rabbi Jonathan Sacks, at the heart of the Hebrew Bible is the claim that 'to love God and to love one's fellow human are indivisible' (2020: 271).

Similarly, a Christian could foreground many themes within the New Testament. One could, for example, place spiritual warfare (Eph. 6:10–20) or an apocalyptic struggle (Rev. 17–19) at the centre of faith and practice. However, many Christians, especially critics of violence, emphasise the Sermon on the Mount as the 'core' of Jesus' message. For these root-oriented Christians, radical faith necessitates turning the cheek, loving enemies and caring for the needy (Matt. 5–7).

Martin Luther King Jr. subverted the idea of moderation and extremism. His 'Letter from a Birmingham Jail' (16 April 1963) responded to Christian and Jewish leaders who urged caution and patience. King was 'gravely disappointed with the white moderate' who blocked the progress of rights. The moderate 'prefers a negative peace which is the absence of tension to a positive peace which is the presence of justice. ... Lukewarm acceptance [of the Civil Rights cause] is much more bewildering than outright rejection'.

Moderate religious leaders considered King's tactics to be extreme. King initially recoiled. Was *he* an extremist?

> But as I continue to think about the matter, I gradually gained a bit of satisfaction from being considered an extremist. Was not Jesus an extremist in love? – 'Love your enemies, bless them that curse you, pray for them that despitefully use you.' Was not Amos an extremist for justice? – 'Let justice roll down like waters and righteousness like a mighty stream.' ... So the question is not whether we will be extremist, but what kind of extremists we will be. Will we be extremists for hate, or will we be extremists for love? Will we be extremists for the preservation of injustice, or will we be extremists for the cause of justice? (King 1963)

King's extremism took the form of principled non-violence coupled with direct action in the pursuit of changing laws and hearts. Commenting on this passage, Patrick Q. Mason frames 'the civil rights movement as a battle of competing religious militancies, ranging from the radically nonviolent to the heinously violent' (2015: 221). On both sides of civil rights, there was 'total commitment, ultimate concern, and complete willingness to sacrifice their own lives if necessary in a righteous cause' (2015: 225). This notion of 'competing religious militancies' needs further elaboration.

5.4 Non-violent Religious Militants

One of the scholarly approaches outlined in Section 2 stressed how religion could lead to several different stances towards violence (the 'ambivalence of the sacred'). This phrase traces to R. Scott Appleby's book by that title. He challenges simplistic and reductionistic approaches to conflict by arguing that religion sometimes limits violence and, at other times, legitimises it. Scholars should not try to erase this tension or pretend it does not exist. Appleby asks deeper questions: why do some religious actors practice their faith in ways that limit conflict and bring about reconciliation when others in the same faith tradition practice their faith in ways that intensify conflict? One might answer that moderate religion leads to peace and radical religion to violence, but Appleby cautions against such approaches.

The sacred often makes ultimate or supreme demands on believers. It is natural, then, that believers act on their faith with a fervency that might be called militancy. Religious militancy refers to the level of commitment, not necessarily to beliefs about a particular lethal act (Mason 2015: 214). A religious militant can be orientated towards violence or away from it. Religious militants have done great harm. However, Appleby argues there are also 'religious militants' who direct their 'sacred rage' against discrimination, unjust policies, government corruption, environmental degradation and the violation of human rights.

> Rather than demonize their opponents, however, these militant believers hope to be reconciled to them and seek to prevent the familiar slide from conflict into violence. Thus they focus rage at execrable acts and policies, not at 'peoples' as a class or tribe or community. They plumb their respective traditions for spiritual and theological insights and practices useful in preventing deadly conflict or limiting its spread. (Appleby 2000: 6–7)

A religious militant can go to the 'extremes' of sanctifying violence or resisting it (Appleby 2000: 11). Religious militants violate human rights and are some of the most stalwart defenders of these rights (Mason 2015: 214). Who is more radical? Appleby argues that 'it should be clear that the peacemaker is no less passionate, no less "radical," than the extremist; indeed, one could argue that the militant peacemaker's rejection of violence as a means of achieving political goals is the more strenuous and radical path' (2000: 13).

This 'plumbing' of faith traditions is important. Religious militants for peace need a firm grounding from which they can confront people – many of them co-religionists – who glorify violence. The intensity of conviction is a key element to their resolve:

> Contrary to the misconceptions popular in some academic and political circles, religious actors play this critical and positive role in world affairs not when they moderate their religion or marginalize their deeply held, vividly symbolized, and often highly particular beliefs in a higher order of love and justice. Religious actors make a difference when they remain religious actors. (Appleby 2012: 248)

This conflict-filled world should prize the 'vast untapped potential of benevolent religious "militants for peace"' (Appleby 2012: 249).

There is a struggle between the two religious militancies. It would be tempting for third parties to argue for one 'authentic' religious expression while (counterproductively) demonising the other. However, Mason notes how the fight is best fought 'within each individual tradition, often at the local level of the church, the synagogue, the mosque, or the temple'. From within,

> peacebuilding militants must be able to mount a convincing, even over-whelming, argument, based squarely on the theology, ritual, and ethics of their particular tradition, that will resonate with the faithful majority of religious leaders and laity who have not had the training or occasion to think deeply about these issues and who can otherwise be swayed by the seductive logic of violence in a moment of crisis. In doing so, they must seriously engage the rhetoric, symbols, and narratives that are invoked by violent militants in convincing fellow believers that theirs is God's cause. (Mason 2015: 227)

Those trying to make 'convincing' arguments cannot ignore 'problematic texts' through a process of selective reading. Rather, their arguments must 'acknowledge with brutal honesty the blood and violence within one's own tradition, rather than avoiding it or shamefully shoving it into the closet' (Mason 2015: 227).

Militant peacemakers are not necessarily pacifists. Although peacemakers share a common disdain for violence, they are not united in the absolute rejection of lethal force (Little 2007: 436–7). Some may deem lethal force a last resort when grave issues of human dignity are at stake, aiming at the end of violence and renewed peaceful coexistence with the enemy (Appleby 2000: 12–13).

In this view, the human response to the sacred is part of the problem and part of the solution. Appleby refutes 'the notion that religion, having so often inspired, legitimated, and exacerbated deadly conflicts, cannot be expected to contribute consistently to their peaceful resolution' (Appleby 2000: 7). The contours of 'religious peacebuilding' are more thoroughly worked out in his co-edited *Oxford Handbook of Religion, Conflict and Peacebuilding*. Appleby's approach focuses on the agency of individuals and groups: 'Simply put, we want to understand why some people acting in sincere response to the sacred – acting religiously – choose violence over nonviolence, death over life' (Appleby 2000: 27). Individuals and communities bear responsibility for how they act on their beliefs and traditions.

5.5 Portrait of Religious Peacemakers

Religious history is a story of division and fragmentation (between faiths and within faiths). This conflict often turns lethal. Intriguingly, non-violent or pacifist-leaning movements often grow out of fervent belief, and sometimes from a faith infused with eschatological expectancy. The 'moderate' often respond lethally to 'fanatical' millenarian peacemaking faiths. For example, even as the Protestant Reformation was descending into confessional war, some strands of Anabaptism completely rejected the use of force. Over a century later, the Quaker movement grew out of the religious fervency of the Puritan revolution. The non-violence of both groups was deemed threatening, and adherents were persecuted. The non-violent Jehovah's Witnesses continue to suffer, and their faith is illegal in much of the world. Similarly, the Bahá'í faith grew out of the Twelver strand of Shia Islam in Iran, and the Iranian government has oppressed the movement for the better part of two centuries (Stockman 2020). There are many more possible relationships between fervent faith and the limitation of violence, most notably the total rejection of all forms of killing in Jainism (Chapple 2011: 263–70).

Some faith communities vigorously promote peace, but individuals within faith traditions often emerge as spokespersons for peace. Appleby notes the importance of Gandhi and Martin Luther King Jr. on generations of famous peace activists and also highlights lesser-known figures whose faith promoted peace. For example, he describes Muslims who argued for the extension of freedom and toleration; who critiqued discrimination against non-Muslims; who promoted human dignity and rights. His scholarship also describes peacemakers within Judaism, Christianity, Hinduism, Buddhism and other religious traditions (2000: 120–280).

Marc Gopin has decades of first-hand experience with peacemakers and offers a portrait of their personalities, methods and motivations. In *Bridges Across an Impossible Divide: The Inner Lives of Arab and Jewish Peacemakers* (2012), he described those who work across one of the world's most volatile fault lines. These peacemakers seem unremarkable, and few have garnered national or international attention. Likening them to life-saving microbes, he notes the 'centrality of positive, almost microscopic increments toward more love, less mutually inflicted suffering, and toward the greater good' (198). For various reasons, each peacemaker reaches across the divide. Gopin notes the similarities between what he calls 'peacemakers and warriors', and some of the best peacemakers were formerly warriors (Gopin 2012: 185).

Peacemakers tend to see networking, hospitality and generosity as part of their religious practice. When networking, they show remarkable flexibility in their 'relationships, strategies, and plans'. They tend to be humorous, take responsibility and pursue their ends with courage, independence and 'evangelical passion'. They are also inquisitive and desire 'to know the whole truth wherever it leads'. Paradoxically, they build their call for 'universal love' on a 'strong sense of ethnic roots'. They promote 'loving land as a basis for healing and unity rather than division' – and this approach is just one of the many ways they advocate 'love and the way of the heart as the key to peace'. Many of these features, like an appreciation for ethnic roots or devotion to the land, are frequently weaponised. However, peacemakers make ethnicity and land serve reconciliation. Peacemakers cultivate patience and 'the suspension of judge-ment' even as they embrace self-criticism. These attitudes promote a deep relationship with religious 'others'. They value 'emotional honesty' as they practice 'deep listening as a way of being with others'. Peacemakers desire to create bridges across warring factions, leading them to emphasise shared values and praise the good they see in adversaries. Finally, they prize 'long-term engagement with adversaries' and show 'faith in the value of ongoing debate and slow and steady influence' (Gopin 2012: 186).

David Little draws a complementary portrait in *Peacemakers in Action* (2007). Peacemakers are often deeply embedded in a community, yet they feel isolated. They tend to emphasise the value of all humanity, show mature emotional intelligence, value self-reflection, possess a well-defined sense of purpose, embrace innovative tactics and find in their religious tradition a deep reservoir of inspiration and strength (2007: 6–9). 'They relentlessly seek recon-ciliation among divided and hostile people – an irreducibly religious undertak-ing' (2007: 21).

6 How Shall We Respond to Violence?

I argued earlier that readers would benefit most from this Element if they adopted five attitudes: curiosity, humility, empathy, charity and self-criticism. They are among the cardinal academic virtues. *Curiosity* is important because we should want to know what motivates people to do awe-inspiring things (and 'awe' encompasses the good and the bad). *Humility* is indispensable. If studying outsiders' failures makes us prideful, we might be better off not knowing their faults. Hubris is counterproductive in conflict situations. *Empathy* is valuable because it is an important tool in understanding the beliefs and motives of those we disagree with. It sharpens critique as we better understand why people act as they do. *Charity*. When we try to treat other people's beliefs with the same care and nuance we treat our own, we can gain a greater insight into why they find such beliefs attractive. Finally, *self-criticism* is necessary because every old and large group (religious or irreligious) has unflattering moments in the past. It is commendable when people squarely face the grim moments in their cherished tradition.

Self-criticism is particularly important. 'I have concluded after decades of observation', writes Marc Gopin, 'that a central source of endless conflict and misery between enemies – but also a central source of misery in families and communities – is the emotional, cognitive, and ethical failure to be self-examined' (2012: 6). Religious traditions have many resources for self-critical faith (Mikva 2020). Indeed, Gopin argues that the confession of personal sin 'combines seamlessly with a willingness culturally to admit the possibility of personal and collective errors' (Gopin 2002: 94). Self-critique and a disposition to doubt might temper some of the dangerous potential in religion and irreligion.

Communities in the present – be they religious or secular – may not be able to completely prevent a portion of their community from harmfully acting on beliefs. However, communities can articulate why such actions cut against their convictions. They can take responsibility for their *reaction* to harm done in the name of their community, and it is based on this reaction that the larger community can be judged. We need more Hindus willing to critique Hindus, Christians willing to critique Christians, Muslims willing to critique Muslims, atheists willing to critique atheists.

6.1 Confronting a Complicated Past

How might individuals and communities bear responsibility for their traditions and beliefs while also responding to those whose violent actions find justification for similar religious beliefs? Should religious groups take responsibility for the actions of co-religionists around the world? Should they take responsibility for the actions of co-religionists in previous centuries? What might 'taking responsibility' look like? The answer often depends on the nature and history of the group.

Newer movements face the problem of novelty; older movements the problem of antiquity. Newer movements often claim to break with the past. Why should anyone believe this new and often small collective possesses knowledge about ultimate truth (the problem of novelty)? Newer movements also have a luxury that more established religions do not have: they do not have to reckon with thousands of years of unflattering history (the problem of antiquity).

New movements often creatively and selectively borrow from previous traditions and they sometimes turn violent. Heaven's Gate, the group that timed mass suicide with celestial objects, propounded novel beliefs that mixed new-age postmodernism, UFOlogy and science fiction with a dash of idiosyncratic Christian interpretation (Chryssides 2016: 2–3). Aum Shinrikyo, the Japanese terrorist group, adapted and blended ideas from a wide range of sources and conspiracy theories, even as they primarily identified with Buddhism (Reader 2000: 68). Groups like Heaven's Gate and Aum Shinrikyo primarily distance themselves from traditional religion. The major religious faiths do not claim responsibility for the beliefs and actions of Heaven's Gate, and the members of Heaven's Gate would not claim responsibility for the violence perpetrated by traditional faiths.

In contrast to newer religious movements, most religious difference stems from splintering from larger and older religions. When splintering happens, the proximity to that larger tradition allows newer denominations or sects to lay claim to the past selectively. Splinter groups can identify with what is good in that history, even as the theological distance helps them disown the bad (solving some of the tensions between novelty and antiquity). Protestant Christians, for example, do not generally feel responsible for the Roman Catholic Inquisition. American Baptists, a subset of Protestants, generally do not feel responsible for Martin Luther's anti-Semitism. And Northern American Baptists do not generally feel personally responsible for the pro-slavery theology of their southern co-religionists. Feelings of responsibility for the past often narrow as group identity narrows.

When opponents of formal religion organised politically during the Enlightenment, they also had the sense of doing something new (even as they borrowed language, imagery and aspirations from Christianity). On the other end of the reign of terror and a long history of irreligious totalitarianism and cultural imperialism, secularism holds a tenuous claim on being novel or less violent. In *Dangerous Religious Ideas*, Rachel Mikva notes how 'secular humanism has been the reigning ideology of nations that pursue conquest and even genocide. Muslim leaders are regularly called upon to renounce the dangers of Islamism, but liberalism is not subjected to the same critique, even though it can also be accused of cultural totalitarianism and violence' because it has a long history of forcing its values and practices on unreceptive peoples (2020: 165). Like their religious counterparts, many secularists have difficulty owning the violence in their own tradition.

All old and large groups have complicated histories. Some chapters of their past might be admirable, others lamentable. There are often large gaps in the story that religious or irreligious groups tell about themselves, and collective memory often involves an element of invention and amnesia. Historical reflection is often divisive. Some group members may remember certain aspects of the past; events and ideas that others in the same group would prefer to forget. However, historical reflection can also be used to bridge some of the divide, provided people actively seek more overlap in what details they remember. The primary divide is between those who want to restore past greatness and those who think time is better spent critiquing the unflattering moments in history (Rowley 2020).

Some who gaze on the religious past see a period of former greatness. Often the history of the nation itself become sacred, and national histories usually involve violence. Thus, historical critique can be tantamount to critiquing the nation in the present. Those who want to restore greatness fear that those who criticise the past want to destroy what is good and praiseworthy. Change tends to be experienced as a cultural and religious loss, unless that change takes the form of restoration. Christians might fondly remember the unchallenged supremacy of Christendom or a more recent moment when the Bible held greater political sway. Muslims might yearn for the restoration of a gilded empire or for a more recent time when the forces of globalisation did not disrupt traditional authority, beliefs and practices. Hindus might reminisce about an age before colonialism or a time when the nation had greater religious homogeneity. Secularists, too, can idealise a time when their ideas were ascendent and religious beliefs had little influence in the public sphere. In each case, an idealised period for one group would be less than ideal for another.

Historical reflection can prompt another reaction, lamentation. Some people are revolted by their faith tradition, abandoning faith altogether or converting to another tradition. However, many critics remain within the faith community. They try to unravel self-congratulatory historical myths from within, and they worry that their faith community will continue to make mistakes if they are unwilling to confront their past. They might emphasise the negative, almost to the exclusion of anything positive. They hope this overwhelmingly negative approach to the past will foster reckoning and renewal. The past is primarily a reservoir of negative examples, and the future for their faith community requires breaking with it. They tend to view change as progress and decry those who want to maintain the status quo or turn the clock backwards. They fear that praising past ages will lead to glorifying all the evil found there.

As a third response, some blend the two earlier approaches. Those adopting this approach fully acknowledge historical wrongs perpetrated by those who shared similar beliefs, deeply and consistently lamenting these wrongs. They argue that it is important to remember these grim moments and understand how they grew out of the faith (even as some may attribute it to a perverted form of their faith). Indeed, these people criticise what they cherish. However, they take an additional step beyond lamentation. Although the repulsive aspects of the past are legion, positive aspects of the past should also be remembered and rehearsed. The path forward involves moving beyond lamentation. Progress requires appreciating and praising what is best in their religious history. The past is a reservoir of both negative and positive examples. They hold history in tension, finding tools in the past – in deeply flawed individuals, institutions and events – and these tools can be used to better the faith community.

This third approach seems conducive to deeply valuing one's faith community while learning from its shortcomings. Self-critical appreciation for the past might also foster a humble and charitable attitude towards theological outsiders whose group also has a complicated past and present. In addition to remembering a more nuanced approach to the good and bad in history, it is important to learn how to confess history and connect the historical dots.

6.2 Confessing the Past; Connecting the Dots

What does it mean to confess the past? The 'confession' spoken of here is not primarily a confession of guilt ('We are personally responsible') but more akin to a confession of faith ('We believe'). Sometimes the first type of confession is necessary. One person might confess personal Islamophobia after 9/11. Another person might confess prejudice towards Jewish people in the United Kingdom, a hatred they felt was justified by Israel's treatment of Palestinians.

When dealing with the wrongs of 'deep history' – wrongs that are so old that all or most living humans cannot be held personally responsible for them – a second type of confession is needed. This confession ('We believe') acknowledges what happened in the past, particularly the harmful acts justified in the name of one's faith community. It is relatively easy to talk about the wrongs of another's tradition. In fact, humans seem hard-wired to remember and rehearse the wrongs done by others: the New Atheists condemn the crimes of the religious; American evangelicals condemn the crimes of Muslims; Islamists condemn the crimes of secular globalism.

It is more challenging to learn about, recall and confess the unflattering moments in one's own history. For example, Christians may confess theological justifications for the slave trade, the close cooperation between missionaries and colonial expansion or a long history of anti-Semitism ('We believe people in our tradition did these things'). The person confessing this history is acknowledging that 'these things happened'. They happened and belong in the story that Christians tell about their past. Confession reconnects past and present injustice. Christians can also confess the good by taking pride in historical believers who vigorously promoted human equality, rights and flourishing.

Confessing the past involves remembering details. Connecting the dots arranges the details into a narrative. The history of one's faith tradition, the good and the bad, is not quarantined from the present. It is relatively easy to remember how the historical failures of an outside religious group impact the present, but it is harder to remember the same about one's faith tradition. Consider the three examples from Christian history mentioned in the previous paragraph: slavery, colonialism and anti-Semitism. To differing degrees, each impacts the present. Where there is anti-Semitism in the present, Christians must be willing to connect the dots into the Christian past. They can also connect the dots for the more positive aspects of their history. For example, one can trace the dots from the rights and privileges enjoyed in many modern Western countries into the Christian past.

6.3 Responding to a Violent Present

If rightly responding to religious violence in the past is important, even more care and nuance is necessary when responding to current violence. Killing places mental demands on onlookers, whether they are personally witnessing the act, reading a newspaper or watching a viral video. It is hard to remain neutral or indifferent. Since we are speaking about human life, it is usually good that humans readily make value judgements.

The threat of violence prompts instant reactions. When, in 2015, a Somalia-based terror group issued a threat against the Mall of America, my mind automatically cycled through responses. I formerly lived nearby and I feared for the safety of my friends. My mind then turned to immigration because there was a large number of Somali refugees in Minneapolis. Should my view of Somali Americans be influenced by threats emanating from Africa? My brain challenged these fears, noting many positive interactions with Somali neighbours. I reminded myself of my conviction that hospitality should outweigh fear. Within seconds, my brain transitioned into international-relations mode, wondering how military force might overpower terrorists in Africa. I then transitioned to a feeling of disgust. This group threatened to terrorise a place set apart for shopping and pleasure, a capitalist sacred ground. Then a sense of vulnerability kicked in as I remembered how quickly a terrorist could shatter my peaceful life. This vulnerability then led to empathy with those around the world whose lives are destroyed by terror groups, or 'collaterally', by those fighting to bring terror to an end.

When I heard this threat, I did not *choose* to respond. Ideas barged into my mind. Thoughts were pulled in contradictory directions. It was difficult to subdue knee-jerk reactions. However, I knew that I could not let involuntary responses reign unchecked. Unregulated responses would lead me to view Somali Americans in ways that were incorrect, biased, unloving and counterproductive.

I assume that we all respond to violence and extremism. Writing this Element is one response; reading it is another. The word 'responding' needs explanation. When most people think of responding to violence, they think of the police, the military or foreign policy. Thankfully, some people think through how to respond from these angles. I suspect most readers of this Element will not be in such a position. I am also not speaking of how those who have been deeply and directly wronged by violence might respond (see works like Gopin 2012).

I am speaking of responding in another sense. How should we respond intellectually and emotionally when we hear of violence or the threat of violence? How should we form beliefs regarding violence perpetrated in God's name? For the sake of peace, how can we criticise our own thoughts? Although thoughts of violence are ever before us, I suspect that we seldom think about our thoughts on religion and violence. In the following I offer guidelines for thinking about killing in God's name. If this killing is a complex phenomenon and oversimplification further jeopardises peace (Rowley 2014), our response should be complex and nuanced (Little 2007: 448).

- Do not think violence is only committed by people with 'other' beliefs.
- Seek out stories that challenge your biases about religion or irreligion.
- Allow your group to be criticised and seek out accounts about harm done by your group.
- Compare like with like: the best in one tradition with the best in another; the worst in one tradition with the worst in another.
- Do not use increased knowledge about religious violence to demonise or misrepresent.
- Do not exaggerate or dismiss the role of sacred beliefs or texts.
- Do not assume there is a necessary connection between most theological beliefs and violent behaviour, and consider how these beliefs can also lead people away from violence.
- Be alert to the possibility that there are spoken and unspoken causes, motives and justifications for violence.
- Be alert to the possibility that justifications and rhetoric change during a conflict.
- Aim at a helpful, gracious, honest and nuanced account of a perpetrator's motivations, not at political correctness.
- Be alert to how groups often radicalise in response to outsiders' hostile attitudes and actions and avoid needlessly making religious groups feel like they live in a hostile environment.
- Resist building peace through shaming outsiders: a sense of shame often fuels resentment between groups, and preserving an opponent's dignity provides a firm foundation for peace.
- Do not treat responsibility for violence as a zero-sum pie because more than one group can bear significant responsibility for a situation that has turned violent.
- Carefully parse the relationship between response and responsibility because violence often comes in response to a non-violent provocation, but the violent still bear responsibility for choosing a lethal response.

- Remember that individuals and communities bear responsibility for how they act on their beliefs and traditions.
- Remember that communities may not be able to prevent some co-religionists from committing harm, but they can articulate why those actions cut against their convictions.
- Resist turning stories of war or conflict into a story about yourself, your political or religious tribe or your pet cause because such inwardness often short-circuits the process of empathising with or helping those who are directly impacted.
- Consider when and why violence shocks us and actively try to expand our empathetic horizon so that we are concerned about a greater variety of conflicts worldwide.

6.4 Toward a Future with Less Conflict

Many fights in the history of religious conflict have been over weighty matters. What obligations do humans have towards each other? What should be done when rights are violated? How can one best love their God and their neighbour? This history also reveals continual fighting over trivial matters; over the theological equivalent of the colour of the carpet. It is easy to look at such conflicts and ask, 'why would someone fight over *that* belief?'

How do we in the present compare? There are certainly weighty things to fight over. How should nations interact? What rights do refugees have? How should resources be divided? How do we address the lingering effects of injustice? Whose voice counts when answering these questions?

However, modern outrage is often aimed at winning a war of attrition over trivial points. But even trivial points can harm when mounted onto a projectile. There are plenty of things to be properly outraged about, but a resounding note in the present is ever-increasing outrage over ever-decreasing stakes. Outrage forestalls curiosity (Ripley 2021: 28). Our climate of outrage is fixated on identifying and denouncing enemies and driving them from our midst (especially from digital congregations). Jonathan Haidt has recently described social media as the distribution of one billion dart guns, and culture incentivises the spraying of darts. Individually, these darts cause 'pain but no fatalities', but we should not underestimate the cumulative effect of hundreds, thousands or millions of dart guns all trained on the same target (2022). Some leaders consolidate power by intensifying conflict. We must become more skilled at identifying 'conflict entrepreneurs' and refusing to amplify their divisive message (Ripley 2021).

Political and social conflicts occupy the news cycle, but religious animosity is ubiquitous. Stephen Pihlaja has written on how Christians, Muslims and atheists evangelise on digital platforms. In the conclusion, he makes a sobering statement: 'It appears impossible to present religious faith online without some amount of immediate, antagonistic response' (2018: 150). When it comes to demonising and despising those we disagree with, I fear the present age has little right to claim the moral high ground.

Our use of words as weapons shows that language matters. But the almost careless way hateful words are typed, liked and shared might also indicate that we do not take our words seriously enough. The novelist and essayist Marilynne Robinson wrote about a Puritan who had a peculiar view of the importance of words. This Puritan hypothesised that God would judge humans twice: the first time when they died and the second time when the consequences of their actions and words played out. Robinson then reflects: 'Someone must have been the first to say that Jews poison wells and cause plague'. In this Puritan's view of divine judgement, the penalties for this anti-Semitic lie are still accruing centuries later (2018: 301).

The reader of this Element may or may not believe in God or divine judgement. The point is that Robinson rightly highlights the durability, adaptability and contagious nature of hateful words and ideas, as well as their dire consequences. Each religious or non-religious group is tempted to cultivate 'respectable' prejudices. Well-poisoning Jews are only one of the innumerable ways that religious or non-religious 'others' have been demonised or dehumanised. Around and around the world, hateful words and ideas go, being adopted and adapted by new people against new people. Each person is a conduit for ideas and beliefs about 'outsiders'. The question is, what kinds of beliefs are allowed to pass through?

When faced with large problems like extremism and violence in God's name, it seems underwhelming to offer small-scale recommendations like curiosity, self-criticism, humility, empathy and charity. However, attitudes about nations are formed around the dinner table in the stories we tell our children about people groups who are not there. Civility is cultivated in our friend groups in how we talk about people holding unfashionable convictions. A complex view of the world is fostered in online communities when we refuse to believe the worst about the motives and intentions of average people of a different faith.

If we live in a democracy, we should reward politicians of conviction who also charitably interact with the other side. If we are part of a religious community, we should highlight elements within our traditions that cultivate respect for all of humanity. If we consume media, we should prioritise outlets that facilitate healthy debate and 'complicate the narrative' when controversial issues are discussed (Ripley 2021). If we are in academia, we should encourage scholarship that fairly represents viewpoints that cut against 'educated' opinion.

Yes, people should have convictions about religious truth. Yes, they should have convictions about what is and is not the best public policy – particularly when choices harm the marginalised or voiceless. But as one hand firmly grasps convictions, the other should be open and willing to try to understand where the modern 'other' is coming from.

In our age of religious, political and social polarisation, we should resist becoming enemy-making machines. The struggle for political and religious purity usually starts by executing charity, humility, self-criticism and genuine diversity. In our limited spheres of influence, we must not allow that to happen. If the history of religious violence teaches anything, it is that we should be wary of trying to remake the world in our own image.

The words we say about the 'other' are part of an inherited discourse that stretches back centuries. Future generations will inherit the enmity that saturates our society. Through small acts of humanity, hopefully, they can also inherit our charity.

References

Achoulias, Marion (2016). Discourse of Sacrifice: Religious Studies and Violence Against Animals. In André Gagné, Spyridon Loumakis and Calogero A. Miceli, eds., *The Global Impact of Religious Violence*, Eugene, OR: Wipf & Stock, 84–113.

Akyol, Mustafa (2011). *Islam Without Extremes: A Muslim Case for Liberty*, New York: W. W. Norton.

Allman, Mark (2008). *Who Would Jesus Kill? War, Peace, and the Christian Tradition*, Winona, MN: Anslem.

Antony, Louise M. (2007). Introduction. In Louise M. Antony, ed., *Philosophers Without Gods: Meditations on Atheism and the Secular Life*, Oxford: Oxford University Press, ix–xiv.

Appleby, Robert Scott (2000). *The Ambivalence of the Sacred: Religion, Violence, and Reconciliation*, New York: Rowman & Littlefield.

(2012). Religion and Global Affairs: Religious 'Militants for Peace'. In Dennis R. Hoover and Douglas M. Johnston, eds., *Religion and Foreign Affairs: Essential Readings*, Waco, TX: Baylor University Press, 245–50.

Armstrong, Karen (2014). *Fields of Blood: Religion and the History of Violence*, London: Bodley Head.

Atwill, David G. (2007). Holy Culture Wars: Patterns of Ethno-Religious Violence in Nineteenth and Twentieth-Century China. In James K. Wellmam, Jr., ed., *Belief and Bloodshed: Religion and Violence across Time and Tradition*, New York: Rowman and Littlefield, 115–29.

Avalos, Hector (2005). *Fighting Words: The Origins of Religious Violence*, Amherst, NY: Prometheus.

Bainton, Roland (1960). *Christian Attitudes Towards War and Peace: A Historical Survey and Critical Reevaluation*, New York: Abingdon.

Baker, Joseph O. and Buster G. Smith (2015). *American Secularism: Cultural Contours of Nonreligious Belief Systems*, London: New York University Press.

Banner, Stuart (2002). *Death Penalty: An American History*, Cambridge, MA: Harvard University Press.

BBC News (2017). Who Was Texas Church Gunman Devin Patrick Kelley? www.bbc.co.uk/news/world-us-canada-41884342.

Belew, Kathleen (2018). *Bring the War Home: The White Power Movement and Paramilitary America*, Cambridge, MA: Harvard University Press.

Berger, J. M. (2018). *Extremism*, Cambridge, MA: MIT Press.

Berger, Peter L. (2007). Secularization Falsified. Paper delivered at the New School for Social Research, William Phillips Memorial Lecture.

Bergmann, Michael, Michael Murray and Michael Rae (2011). Introduction. In *Divine Evil? The Moral Character of the God of Abraham*, Oxford: Oxford University Press, 1–19.

Berlinerblau, Jacques (2005). *The Secular Bible: Why Nonbelievers Must Take Religion Seriously*, Cambridge: Cambridge University Press.

(2022). *Secularism: The Basics*. London: Routledge.

Bessel, Richard (2015), *Violence: A Modern Obsession*, London: Simon & Schuster.

Birdsall, Judd and Drew Collins (2017). Reconsidering Religious Radicalism, *The Review of Faith and International Affairs*, 15(2), 1–4.

Birdsall, Judd and Matthew Rowley (2019). Stop Weaponizing the Bible for Trump: No Politician Is a Cyrus, David or Caesar, *Washington Post*.

Blackburn, Simon (2007). Religion and Respect. In Louise M. Antony, ed., *Philosophers without Gods: Meditations on Atheism and the Secular Life*, Oxford: Oxford University Press, 179–93.

Brown, Jonathan A. C. (2016). Sin, Forgiveness, and Reconciliation: A Muslim Perspective. In Lucinda Mosher and David Marshal, eds., *Sin, Forgiveness and Reconciliation: Christian and Muslim Perspectives*, Washington, DC: Georgetown University Press, 13–19.

Buc, Philippe (2015). *Holy War, Martyrdom, and Terror: Christianity, Violence, and the West*, Philadelphia: University of Pennsylvania Press.

Burke, Edmund (1790). *Reflections on the Revolution in France*, 2nd ed., London: J. Dodsley, 1790.

Burns, Charlene (2008). *More Moral than God: Taking Responsibility for Religious Violence*, Lanham, MD: Rowman & Littlefield.

Carlson, John D. (2011). Religion and Violence: Coming to Terms with Terms. In Andrew R. Murphy, ed., *The Blackwell Companion to Religion and Violence*, Oxford: Blackwell, 7–22.

Carlson, John D. and Jonathan H. Ebel (2012). Introduction: John Brown, Jeremiad, and Jihad: Reflections on Religion, Violence, and America. In John D. Carlson and Jonathan H. Ebel, eds., *Jeremiad to Jihad: Religion, Violence, and America*, Berkeley: University of California Press, 1–25.

Cavanaugh, William (2009). *The Myth of Religious Violence: Secular Ideology and the Roots of Modern Conflict*, Oxford: Oxford University Press.

Chapple, Christopher Key (2011). The Dialectic of Violence in Jainism. In Andrew R. Murphy, ed., *The Blackwell Companion to Religion and Violence*, Oxford: Blackwell, 263–70.

Chryssides, George D. (2016). Approaching Heaven's Gate. In George D. Chryssides, ed., *Heaven's Gate: Postmodernity and Popular Culture in a Suicide Group*, repr., New York: Routledge, 1–16.

Clarke, Steve (2014). *The Justification of Religious Violence*, Chichester: Wiley Blackwell.

Coffey, John (2014). *Exodus and Liberation: Deliverance Politics from John Calvin to Martin Luther King Jr.*, Oxford: Oxford University Press.

Cremer, Tobias (2018). Defenders of the Faith: Why Right-Wing Populists Are Embracing Religion, *The New Statesman*. www.newstatesman.com/polit ics/religion/2018/05/defenders-faith-0.

Das, Veena (2013). Violence and Nonviolence at the Heart of Hindu Ethics. In Michael Jerryson, Mark Juergensmeyer, and Margo Kitts, eds., *The Oxford Handbook of Religion and Violence*, Oxford: Oxford University Press, 15–40.

Dawkins, Richard (2006). *The God Delusion*, Boston, MA: Houghton Mifflin.

Dawson, Lorne L. (2006). Psychopathologies and the Attribution of Charisma: A Critical Introduction to the Psychology of Charisma and the Explanation of Violence in New Religious Movements. *Nova Religio*, 10, 3–28.

Dennett, Daniel C. (2006). *Breaking the Spell: Religion as a Natural Phenomenon*, London: Penguin.

Eisen, Robert (2011). *The Peace and Violence of Judaism: From the Bible to Modern Zionism*, Oxford: Oxford University Press.

Ellens, Jay Harold (2004). Fundamentalism, Orthodoxy, and Violence. In J. Harold Ellens, ed., *The Destructive Power of Religion: Violence in Judaism, Christianity, and Islam*, vol. 4, Westport, CT: Praeger, 119–42.

Eller, Jack David (2010). *Cruel Creeds, Virtuous Violence: Religious Violence Across Culture and History*, Amherst, MA: Prometheus.

Enns, Diane (2012). *The Violence of Victimhood*, University Park: Pennsylvania State University Press.

Fiske, Alan Page and Tage Shakti Rai (2015). *Virtuous Violence*, Cambridge: Cambridge University Press.

Forst, Brian (2009). *Terrorism, Crime, and Public Policy*, Cambridge: Cambridge University Press.

Foster, Russell, Nick Megoran and Michael Dunn (2017). Towards a Geopolitics of Atheism: Critical Geopolitics Post the 'War on Terror'. *Political Geography*, 60, 179–89.

Fulford, Ben (2017). Moderating Religious Identity and the Eclipse of Religious Wisdom: Lessons from Hans Frei. *The Review of Faith and International Affairs*, 15(2), 24–33.

Gagné, Angré (2016). Tyranny of Political Correctness and Religious Violence. In Angré Gagné, Spyridon Loumakis and Calogero A. Miceli, eds., *The Global Impact of Religious Violence*, Eugene, OR: Wipf & Stock, 1–12.

Girard, René (1986). *The Scapegoat*, Yvonne Freccero, trans., Baltimore, MD: Johns Hopkins University Press.

Glazebrook, Trish (2001). Violence against Nature: A Philosophical Perspective. *Journal of Power and Ethics: An Interdisciplinary Review*, 2(4), 322–43.

Goldie, Mark, ed., (2010). *John Locke: A Letter Concerning Toleration and Other Writings*, Indianapolis, IN: Liberty Fund.

Gopin, Marc (2002). *Holy War, Holy Peace*, Oxford: Oxford University Press.

(2012). *Bridges across an Impossible Divide: The Inner Lives of Arab and Jewish Peacemakers*, Oxford: Oxford University Press.

Gray, John (2018). *Seven Types of Atheism*, London: Allen Lane.

Haidt, Jonathan (2022). Why the Past 10 Years of American Life Have Been Uniquely Stupid, *The Atlantic*. Online: www.theatlantic.com/magazine/archive/2022/05/social-media-democracy-trust-babel/629369/

Hamid, Shadi (2014). *Temptations of Power: Islamists and Illiberal Democracy in a New Middle East*, Oxford: Oxford University Press.

(2016). *Islamic Exceptionalism: How the Struggle Over Islam Is Reshaping the World*, New York: St. Martin's.

(2022). There Are Many Things Worse Than American Power, *The Atlantic*. Online: www.theatlantic.com/ideas/archive/2022/03/putin-kremlin-imperialism-ukraine-american-power/624180/

Harari, Yuval Noah (2017). *Homo Deus: A Brief History of Tomorrow*, New York: Harper.

Harris, Sam (2004). *The End of Faith: Religion, Terror, and the Future of Reason*, New York: W. W. Norton.

Haslam, Nick (2016). Concept Creep: Psychology's Expanding Concept of Harm and Pathology. *Psychological Inquiry*, 27, 1–17.

Hassner, Ron E. (2016). *Religion on the Battlefield*, Ithaca: Cornell University Press.

Hauerwas, Stanley (2012). Hauerwas on 'Hauerwas and the Law': Trying to Have Something to Say. *Law and Contemporary Problems*, 75(4), 233–51.

Hibbard, Scott (2015). Religion, Nationalism and the Politics of Secularism. In Atalia Omar, R. Scott Appleby and David Little, eds., *The Oxford Handbook of Religion, Conflict and Peacebuilding*, Oxford: Oxford University Press, 100–23.

Hitchens, Christopher (2007). *God Is Not Great: How Religion Poisons Everything*, repr., New York: Twelve.

Hochschild, Ariel Russell (2016). *Strangers in Their Own Land: Anger and Mourning on the American Right*, New York: New Press.

Holland, Glenn S. (2009). *Gods in the Desert: Religions of the Ancient Near East*, New York: Rowman & Littlefield.

Holley, Joe (2020). *Sutherland Springs: God, Guns, and Hope in a Texas Town*, New York: Hachette Books.

Holzer, Jacob. C. and Emily Threlkeld, William Costanza, Patricia R. Recupero and Samara E. Rainey (2022). Comparing Lone-Actor Terrorism to Other High-Threat Groups. In Jacob C. Halzer et al., eds., *Lone-Actor Terrorism: An Integrated Framework*, Oxford: Oxford University Press, 269–86.

Holzer, Jacob C., Olivia Zurek, and Lauren Simpson, eds. (2022). Case Reviews in Lone-Actor Terrorism Incidents. In Jacob C. Halzer et al., eds., *Lone-Actor Terrorism: An Integrated Framework*, Oxford: Oxford University Press, 23–39.

Horn, Dara (2021). *People Love Dead Jews: Reports from a Haunted Present*, New York: W. W. Norton.

Ingersoll, Julie (2013). Religiously Motivated Violence in the Abortion Debate. In Michael Jerryson, Mark Juergensmeyer, and Margo Kitts, eds., *The Oxford Handbook of Religion and Violence*, Oxford: Oxford University Press, 315–23.

Jakobsen, Janet R. (2004). Is Secularism Less Violent than Religion? In Elizabeth Castelli and Janet R. Jakobsen, eds., *Interventions: Activists and Academics Respond to Violence*, New York, Palgrave Macmillan, 53–67.

Jakobsen, Janet R. and Ann Pellegrini (2008). Introduction: Times Like These. In Janet R. Jakobsen and Ann Pellegrini, eds., *Secularisms*, Durham, NC: Duke University Press, 1–35.

Jenkins, Philip (2012). *Laying Down the Sword: Why We Can't Ignore the Bible's Violent Verses*, New York: HarperOne.

Jerryson, Michael (2013). Buddhist Traditions and Violence. In Michael Jerryson, Mark Juergensmeyer, and Margo Kitts, eds., *The Oxford Handbook of Religion and Violence*, Oxford: Oxford University Press, 41–66.

Johnson, Dominic (2016). *God Is Watching You: How the Fear of God Makes Us Human*, Oxford: Oxford University Press.

Johnson, James Turner (2012). Contemporary Warfare and American Efforts at Restraint. In John D. Carlson and Jonathan H. Ebel, eds., *Jeremiad to Jihad: Religion, Violence, and America*, Berkeley: University of California Press, 233–49.

Jones, James W. (2008). *Blood that Cries Out from the Earth: The Psychology of Religious Terrorism*, Oxford: Oxford University Press.

Juergensmeyer, Mark (2000). *Terror in the Mind of God: The Global Rise of Religious Violence*, Berkeley: University of California Press.

Juergensmeyer, Mark, Margo Kitts, and Michael Jerryson (2013). Introduction: The Enduring Relationship of Religion and Violence. In Michael Jerryson, Mark Juergensmeyer, and Margo Kitts, eds., *The Oxford Handbook of Religion and Violence*, Oxford: Oxford University Press, 1–12.

Kärkkäinen, Veli-Matti (2016). Sin, Forgiveness, and Reconciliation: A Christian Perspective. In Lucinda Mosher and David Marshal, eds., *Sin, Forgiveness and Reconciliation: Christian and Muslim Perspectives*, Washington, DC: Georgetown University Press, 3–12.

Khalil, Mohammad Hassan (2018). *Jihad, Radicalism, and the New Atheism*, Cambridge: Cambridge University Press.

Kimball, Charles (2009). *When Religion Becomes Evil*, New York: Harper Collins.

King Jr., Martin Luther (1963). Letter from the Birmingham Jail. Online: https://library.samford.edu/special/treasures/2013/king-letter-bham-jail.html

LaRocca, Donald J. (1996). *The Gods of War: Sacred Imagery and the Decorations of Arms and Armor*, New York: The Metropolitan Museum of Art.

Lawrence, Bruce B. (2013). Muslim Engagement with Injustice and Violence. In Michael Jerryson, Mark Juergensmeyer, and Margo Kitts, eds., *The Oxford Handbook of Religion and Violence*, Oxford: Oxford University Press, 126–52.

Leadbetter, Bill (1999). Genocide in Antiquity. In Israel W. Charny, ed., *Encyclopedia of Genocide*, vol. 1, Santa Barbara, CA: ABC-CLIO, 273.

Lepore, Jill (1998). *The Name of War: King Phillip's War and the Origins of American Identity*, New York: Knopf.

Lie, John and Jeffrey Wend (2020). East Asia. In John Stone, Rutledge Dennis, Polly Rizova, and Xiaoshuo Hou, eds., *The Wiley Blackwell Companion to Race, Ethnicity, and Nationalism*, Oxford: Wiley Blackwell, 129–46.

Little, David (2007). *Peacemakers in Action: Profiles in Religion and Conflict Resolution*, Cambridge: Cambridge University Press.

Maclear, J. F., ed. (1995). *Church and State in the Modern Age: A Documentary History*, New York: Oxford University Press.

Mahmood, Cynthia Keppley (2013). Sikh Traditions and Violence. In Michael Jerryson, Mark Juergensmeyer, and Margo Kitts, eds., *The Oxford Handbook of Religion and Violence*, Oxford: Oxford University Press, 67–77.

Martin, David (1997). *Does Christianity Cause War?* Vancouver: Regent College Publishing.

——— (2006). *Does Christianity Cause War?* Vancouver: Regent College Publishing.

Mason, Patrick Q. (2015). Violent and Nonviolent Religious Militancy. In Atalia Omar, R. Scott Appleby and David Little, eds., *The Oxford Handbook of Religion, Conflict and Peacebuilding*, Oxford: Oxford University Press, 212–35.

Meral, Ziya (2018). *How Violence Shapes Religion: Belief and Conflict in the Middle East and Africa*, Cambridge: Cambridge University Press.

Mikva, Rachel S. (2020). *Dangerous Religious Ideas: The Deep Roots of Self-Critical Faith in Judaism, Christianity, and Islam*, Boston, MA: Beacon.

Murphy, Andrew R. (1997). Tolerance, Toleration, and the Liberal Tradition, *Polity*, 29 (4), 593–623.

Murphy, James Bernard (2014). Religious Violence: Myth or Reality? A Symposium on William T. Cavanaugh's The Myth of Religious Violence, *Political Theology*, 15(6), 479–85.

Nelson, Eric (2010). *The Hebrew Republic: Jewish Sources and the Transformation of European Political Thought*, Cambridge, MA: Harvard University Press.

New York Times (2009). Obama's Nobel Remarks. Online: www.nytimes.com/ 2009/12/11/world/europe/11prexy.text.html

Nongbri, Brent (2013). *Before Religion: A History of a Modern Concept*, New Haven, CT: Yale University Press.

O'Brien, Conor Cruise (1988). *God Land: Reflections on Religion and Nationalism*, Cambridge, MA: Harvard University Press.

Olsen, Joel (2011). The Politics of Protestant Violence: Abolitionists and Anti-Abortion Activists. In Andrew R. Murphy, ed., *The Blackwell Companion to Religion and Violence*, Oxford: Blackwell, 485–97.

Pfeifer, Birgit and R. Ruard Ganzevoort (2014). The Implicit Religion of School Shootings: Existential Concerns of Perpetrators Prior to Their Crime. *Journal of Religion and Violence*, 2, 447–59.

Pihlaja, Stephen (2018). *Religious Talk Online: The Evangelical Discourse of Muslims, Christians and Atheists*, Cambridge: Cambridge University Press.

Pinker, Stephen (2011). *The Better Angels of Our Nature: A History of Violence and Humanity*, London: Penguin.

——— (2018). *Enlightenment Now: The Case for Reason, Science, Humanism, and Progress*, New York: Viking.

Piven, Jerry S. (2004). On the Psychosis (Religion) of Terrorists. In Chris E. Stout, ed., *The Psychology of Terrorism*, vol. 3, Westport: Praeger, 119–48.

Plato (2017). *Euthyphro. Apology. Crito. Phaedo*. Christopher Emlyn-Jones and William Preddy, ed. and trans., Loeb Classical Library 36, Cambridge, MA: Harvard University Press.

Radner, Ephraim (2012). *A Brutal Unity: The Spiritual Politics of the Christian Church*, Waco, TX: Baylor University Press.

Rahman, Fazlur (2009). *Major Themes of the Qur'an*, 2nd ed., Chicago: University of Chicago Press.

Ratzinger, Joseph (2005). That Which Holds the World Together. In F. Schuller, ed., *Dialectics of Secularization: On Reason and Religion*, B. McNeil, trans., San Francisco, CA: Ignatius Press, 53–80.

Rawls, John (1999). *The Law of Peoples: With 'The Idea of Public Reason Revisited'*, Cambridge, MA: Harvard University Press.

Reader, Ian (2000). *Religious Violence in Contemporary Japan: The Case of Aum Shinrikyō*, Richmond, VA: Curzon.

Reynolds, David S. (2005). *John Brown, Abolitionist: The Man Who Killed Slavery, Sparked the Civil War, and Seeded Civil Rights*, New York: Vintage.

Ripley, Amanda (2021). *High Conflict: Why We Get Trapped and How We Get Out*, New York: Simon & Schuster.

Roberts, Adam and Joshua Cole (2017). Man Who Shot Texas Church Gunman Shares His Story, *40/29 News*. Online: www.4029tv.com/article/man-who-shot-texas-church-gunman-shares-his-story/13437943

Robinson, Marilynne (2018). *What Are We Doing Here?*, New York: Farrar, Straus and Giroux.

Rosenfeld, Gavriel (2018). How Americans Described Evil Before Hitler, *The Atlantic*. Online: www.theatlantic.com/ideas/archive/2018/10/can-we-compare-donald-trump-hitler/572194/

Rowley, Matthew (2014). What Causes Religious Violence? Three Hundred Claimed Contributing Causes, *Journal of Religion and Violence*, 2(3), 361–402.

    (2017). 'All Pretend an Holy War': Radical Beliefs and the Rejection of Persecution in the Mind of Roger Williams, *The Review of Faith & International Affairs*, 15(2), 66–76.

    (2020). *Trump and the Protestant Reaction to Make America Great Again*. London: Routledge.

    (2024). *Godly Violence in the Puritan Atlantic World, 1636–1676: A Study of Military Providentialism*, Woodbridge: Boydell.

Rowley, Matthew and Natasha Hodgson, eds. (2022). *Miracles, Political Authority and Violence in the Medieval and Early Modern Worlds*, London: Routledge.

Sacks, Jonathan (2015). *Not in God's Name: Confronting Religious Violence*, London: Hodder & Stoughton.

(2020). *Morality: Restoring the Common Good in Divided Times*, New York: Basic.

Schwartz, Regina M. (1997). *The Curse of Cain: The Violent Legacy of Monotheism*, Chicago: University of Chicago Press.

Shagan, Ethan H. (2011). *The Rule of Moderation: Violence, Religion and the Politics of Restraint in Early Modern England*, Cambridge: Cambridge University Press.

Shah, Timothy Samuel (2015). Secular Militancy as an Obstacle to Peacebuilding. In Atalia Omar, R. Scott Appleby, and David Little, eds., *The Oxford Handbook of Religion, Conflict and Peacebuilding*, Oxford: Oxford University Press, 380–406.

Shahar, Meir (2013). Violence in Chinese Religious Traditions. In Michael Jerryson, Mark Juergensmeyer, and Margo Kitts, eds., *The Oxford Handbook of Religion and Violence*, Oxford: Oxford University Press, 182–96.

Sinnott-Armstrong, Walter (2007). Overcoming Christianity. In Louise M. Antony, ed., *Philosophers Without Gods: Meditations on Atheism and the Secular Life*, Oxford: Oxford University Press, 69–79.

Skya, Walter A. (2011). Religion, Violence and Shintō. In Andrew R. Murphy, ed., *The Blackwell Companion to Religion and Violence*, Oxford: Blackwell, 227–36.

Slezkine, Yuri (2017). *The House of Government: A Saga of the Russian Revolution*. Princeton, NJ: Princeton University Press.

Smith, Shane (2021). Nuclear Weapons and North Korean Foreign Policy. In Adrian Buzo, ed., *Routledge Handbook of Contemporary North Korea*, New York: Routledge, 141–55.

Soper, J. Christopher and Joel S. Fetzer (2018). *Religion and Nationalism in Global Perspective*. Cambridge: Cambridge University Press.

Stark, Rodney and Katie Corcoran (2014). *Religious Hostility: A Global Assessment of Hatred and Terror*, Waco, TX: ISR Books.

Stockman, Robert H. (2020). *The Bahá'í Faith, Violence, and Non-Violence*, Cambridge: Cambridge University Press.

Stozier, Charles B. and David M. Terman (2010). Introduction. In Charles B. Stozier, David M. Terman and James W. Jones, eds., *The*

Fundamentalist Mindset: Psychological Perspectives on Religion, Violence, and History, Oxford: Oxford University Press, 3–15.

Sue, Derald Wing (2010). *Microaggressions in Everyday Life: Race, Gender, and Sexual Orientation*, Hoboken, NJ: John Wiley & Sons.

Taunton, Larry Alex (2016). *The Faith of Christopher Hitchens: The Restless Soul of the World's Most Notorious Atheist*, Nashville, TN: Thomas Nelson.

Taylor, Charles (2007). *A Secular Age*, Cambridge, MA: Harvard University Press.

Teehan, John (2010). *In the Name of God: The Evolutionary Origins of Religious Ethics and Violence*, Chichester: Wiley-Blackwell.

Thomas, Keith (2018). *In Pursuit of Civility: Manners and Civilization in Early Modern England*, New Haven, CT: Yale University Press.

Trodd, Zoe and John Stauffer (2004). *Meteor of War: The John Brown Story*. Maplecrest, NY: Brandywine.

Volf, Miroslav (2008). Christianity and Violence. In Richard S. Hess and Elmer A. Martens, eds., *War in the Bible and Terrorism in the Twenty-First Century*, Winona Lake, IN: Eisenbrauns, 1–17.

(2015). *Flourishing: Why We Need Religion in a Globalized World*, New Haven, CT: Yale University Press.

Ward, Keith (2006). *Is Religion Dangerous?* Oxford: Eerdmans.

Wielenberg, Erik J. (2013). Atheism and Morality. In Stephen Bullivant and Michael Ruse, eds., *The Oxford Handbook of Atheism*, Oxford: Oxford University Press, 89–103.

Wilson, Stephen M. (2017). Blood Vengeance and the Imago Dei in the Flood Narrative (Genesis 9:6), *Interpretation*, 71(3), 263–73.

Winship, Michael P. (2019). *Hot Protestants: A History of Puritanism in England and America*, London: Yale University Press.

Wlodarczyk, Nathalie (2013). African Traditional Religion and Violence. In Michael Jerryson, Mark Juergensmeyer, and Margo Kitts, eds., *The Oxford Handbook of Religion and Violence*, Oxford: Oxford University Press, 153–66.

Wright, Joshua D. (2016). More Religion, Less Justification for Violence: A Cross-National Analysis, *Archive for the Psychology of Religion*, 38(2), 159–83.

Wuthnow, Robert (2012). *The God Problem: Expressing Faith and Being Reasonable*, Berkeley: University of California Press.

Young, Jeremy (2008). *The Violence of God and the War on Terror*, New York: Seabury.

Zuckerman, Phil (2013). Atheism and Societal Health. In Stephen Bullivant and Michael Ruse, eds., *The Oxford Handbook of Atheism*, Oxford: Oxford University Press, 497–510.

Cambridge Elements ≡

The Problems of God

Series Editor
Michael L. Peterson
Asbury Theological Seminary

Michael L. Peterson is Professor of Philosophy at Asbury Theological Seminary. He is the author of *God and Evil* (Routledge); *Monotheism, Suffering, and Evil* (Cambridge University Press); *With All Your Mind* (University of Notre Dame Press); *C. S. Lewis and the Christian Worldview* (Oxford University Press); *Evil and the Christian God* (Baker Book House); and *Philosophy of Education: Issues and Options* (Intervarsity Press). He is co-author of *Reason and Religious Belief* (Oxford University Press); *Science, Evolution, and Religion: A Debate about Atheism and Theism* (Oxford University Press); and *Biology, Religion, and Philosophy* (Cambridge University Press). He is editor of *The Problem of Evil: Selected Readings* (University of Notre Dame Press). He is co-editor of *Philosophy of Religion: Selected Readings* (Oxford University Press) and *Contemporary Debates in Philosophy of Religion* (Wiley-Blackwell). He served as General Editor of the Blackwell monograph series Exploring Philosophy of Religion and is founding Managing Editor of the journal *Faith and Philosophy.*

About the Series
This series explores problems related to God, such as the human quest for God or gods, contemplation of God, and critique and rejection of God. Concise, authoritative volumes in this series will reflect the methods of a variety of disciplines, including philosophy of religion, theology, religious studies, and sociology.

Cambridge Elements ≡

The Problems of God

Elements in the Series

Printed in the United States
by Baker & Taylor Publisher Services

Printed in the United States
by Baker & Taylor Publisher Services